# SASQUATCH IS OUT THERE

GARY & WENDY SWANSON

Cover design by Jim Myers, The Sasquatch Outpost, Bailey, Colorado


Background photo courtesy of Silviarita on Pixabay





Published by Swanson Literary Group
ISBN:  9798578458798

Other books by the authors:


*They Saw Sasquatch*
*Sasquatch Encounters*
*Bigfoot Uncovered*
*Tracking Sasquatch*
*Sasquatch!: Reports From the Field*
*Bigfoot Adventures*
*On the Trail of Sasquatch*
*Hiking Sasquatch Country: Best Hikes In Southern Oregon*
*Squatchin': Study Guide & Field Handbook for Tracking Sasquatch*

*Skinwalkers Shapeshifters and Native American Curses*
*The Last Skinwalker*
*We Survived Native American Witches, Curses & Skinwalkers*
*Skinwalker: Guardian of the Last Portal*

If ever you are traveling in Colorado and can stop by the Sasquatch Outpost on 149 Main St, Bailey 80421 we would love to meet you, and are always ready to "talk Bigfoot". It is our greatest joy to hear other people's stories, and we now have such a wealth of them, if you ever want to hear one, we will happily start pulling them out of the bag! The trick, I have heard, is to get us to stop!!

You can also find us online at sasquatchoutpost.com or call us at our store on 303-816-9383. And of course, if you have a story of a sighting in Colorado, be sure to come by and put your pin in our map and give us another story to add to our collection.

Happy Squatching everyone!

Jim and Daphne Myers

# CONTENTS

# PREFACE

What kind of people submit these stories? This is a fairly common question that we are often asked by those people who have a Sasquatch story, but are reticent about actually telling it. In publishing our first hiking book, "Hiking Sasquatch Country," we had included a few actual encounters that our friends had experienced during their personal hikes, along with a few of their discoveries about the Bigfoot itself.

It was after that book began selling that we started receiving a flood of personal experiences with this elusive animal from people all across the country; and eventually, we separated our favorite hikes throughout Southern Oregon into its own book and published our best-selling book, "They Saw Sasquatch."

That opened the floodgates so to speak; because, from then on, we began receiving individual reports of hikers and regular visitors to mountains and forests all across the United States and British Columbia. We suddenly had a lot of reports from people who had both seen the Bigfoot, and many of whom experienced personal encounters with these creatures!

Over the years, we have received large numbers of reports of sightings and many actual encounters and we try to get some type of verification from our submitters that they really had an actual experience. Unfortunately, so many of these encounters are almost the same exact scenarios that we cannot include all of the stories we receive. Like our own personal experiences that prompted us to share them in our hiking book, ours were most like the others we have received since we began. This makes sense, as the majority of encounters take place in similar settings, and in the excitement of the moment, many important details go unnoticed.

Stories we publish cannot be proven without further research and we use due diligence in many cases where we request further explanation of "questionable" stories. We use many sources in order to best separate actual events from wishful thinking.

We offer a signed copy of the book in which a submitter's story appears and the only other incentive is they may purchase additional copies for friends and relatives at discounted prices. That is the only incentive we offer, as the fun part of it, according to our growing contributor base, is the lifetime satisfaction of being able to retell the almost unimaginable thrill of a real-life encounter with America's most mysterious creature. Once a person has seen one; you never, ever forget! This is what for most people is a once in a lifetime experience.

Submitters' actual identities are known only to the publishers, and we caution against those who want to use their real names; all personal information is destroyed once the book has been published and they have received their copies.

## INVITATION:

If you have had a personal encounter with, or a sighting of a Sasquatch that you would like to see published in our next book, please send the details and any accompanying photos to:

swanliterary@gmail.com

Thank you and "Happy Squatchin!"

# INTRODUCTION

The stories in this book are reports of actual sightings and encounters by people who were, before these experiences, relative strangers to the Sasquatch.

One select group of Bigfoot researchers actually conducted an organized exploration deep into the Rocky Mountains seeking proof as to whether or not the Bigfoot hibernate. This subject has been highly controversial among Sasquatch researchers, and this particular study from this team of volunteers has reached a conclusion regarding the rather large group of Sasquatch that they selected for their study.

One of the stories selected for this book is from an Oregon beachcomber who was challenged by a Sasquatch for possession of a rare Japanese glass float.

You'll read about the couple, who against their realtor's wishes, sold their home because the Sasquatch family was included in the deal.

We have included a wide variety of Bigfoot stories that came with credible evidence, and we hope you enjoy them as much as we did.

# SASKOT (SASQUATCH)

By Gary Swanson

The local band of native Americans in southern Oregon leave offerings around the base of this tree that was badly burned in a forest fire years ago. Prior to the fire, their people saw the tree as a sacred site according to local native people.

This is how they explained it to us; it is said by the local residents that the indigenous people see several images that they believe are signs from the gods that their people are protected, and they believe the images became plainly visible after the fire of the Saskot. Saskot was one translation given to us, (Native American name for Sasquatch). From the top: A Sasquatch, a bear and a wolf (offerings still appear at times).

Our research into this legend led us to an elderly lady who told us her great grandfather had been an early gold miner in the Oregon mountains, and she had been handed down a collection of handwritten letters that the man had dictated to a man he referenced as a "scribe," that often came prior to the mail carrier.

Our research into these gold rush days indicated in several references that man often referred to as a scribe or "letter writer" by some, was a man who often accompanied the visits with the postman, and he would translate the words from the gold miners into legible letters for a fee, often paid in gold by weight, and the postal rider would also collect his fee in gold, and with his mule or burro, he would dispatch those letters when he reached the railroad in the valley far away.

To this day, they still honor these three sacred images, claiming the images appeared after the forest burned.

The lady said that she also had a "very special" letter, that from the wear on the pages, must have been read very often over the years. Since this letter was penned in the 1800's we did not touch it until we retrieved our cloth gloves from the car, but it was a real thrill to just hold the fraying paper. We were sorry that she wouldn't allow us to photograph the pages, but her explanation was satisfactory, so we concurred.

The transcriber had taken the time to print each word for the sake of clarity, and then it came to a place on the third page where we saw the reason this lady had contacted us in the first place; a definite and carefully worded paragraph that referred directly to the Sasquatch!

There was the word "Sasquit," and it had another word alongside, and it said "Saskot" with question marks after it, as if the scribe, nor the lady's great grandfather weren't sure of the spelling, but then he referred to it as an animal the local Indians were afraid of, like a "booger man" he said.

The letter made reference to a particular tree where the local Indians left offerings of food around, and that tree was where they left offerings to Saskot.

We found little reference to this tree in question, other than the fact that the tribe considered this mighty tree to be a direct route to their gods, and the gold miners knew to stay far away from it.

No one knows for certain what started the forest fire; most people believe that it was caused by lightning, and some stories were that one of the miners had gotten drunk and argued with a couple of tribal members, and it was he who deliberately set the fire, but he had only intended to burn the one single tree, but a sudden windstorm rolled in and tore through the entire mountain, burning for miles through the thick timber. No definite decision was reached, but the miner was never seen again after that fire.

After the devastation burned the entire area, the tribe moved into a pristine forest some five or so miles away, but it is said in several references, that they still paid regular visits to leave offerings at the base of the altar, and the photo indicates the shapes of the spirit gods that they believe have made their images appear so as to tell their people that their prayers are still being heard by the ancient ones.

# SASQUATCH AT WHISKY CREEK ON THE ROGUE RIVER

## By Jean

My name is Jean, and my husband Barney and I have lived in Oregon all of our lives, and we have often hiked the Rogue River Trail beginning at Grave Creek and going toward Marial; our goal being the old cabin at Whisky Creek, that we really enjoy.

The only thing we didn't care for, was the number of hikers that we had to contend with on that horribly narrow cliff! In many areas, you have to walk single file, and often, there will be someone in too much of a hurry, and they try to brush by anyway! With today's backpacks it gets pretty hairy in those places where it's a hundred feet straight down! Especially since we are getting older.

That's why when we purchased your book "Hiking Sasquatch Country," We were astounded to read about your back route over the mountain. We had never before, seen any reference to a back way in and why you mentioned that the government doesn't want people coming in from above. After our trip, we can readily understand why they discourage anyone using that route, because cell phone reception is poor to none at all; that is no problem using the cliff trail with all of the people there; you can always get help.

Even though we have lived in Merlin for the last fifteen years, and have hiked the Rogue countless times, we had only seen a Sasquatch on three occasions; none of them very close.

Whenever we depart from our usual spot at the Grave Creek boat landing, we are in the habit of hiking in as far as the Whisky Creek Cabin, and relaxing there for a while before heading back, which generally takes us six, or eight hours, so we return in daylight, and we always enjoy ourselves.

We read of your experience in one of your other books, where you almost died on your return, and we saw the place you referred to, and could easily understand how it could have been very scary, especially with no more water on that unmercifully hot cliff! We have had similar struggles in that horribly hot canyon.

Anyway, we were really anxious to take your "back way" route, and we were really pleased that the route you gave was so easy to follow. The BLM (Bureau of land Management) gate was locked, and that was good because Barney might have tried to take our Jeep down there, but your warning helped me convince him to pull into the grassy area above the gate and park. I was glad it was locked, as if we had tried driving, we may have found it locked on our way back. With no cell phone reception we would have had a long walk home!

Shouldering our packs, we hit the road, and in fact we hit it several times, as that was the steepest gravel road either of us had ever been on. I know that I personally slid and fell at least six times, and if not for our hiking sticks it would have been many more! I wonder what the forestry people must drive, because Barney said he didn't think our Trailhawk could have made it back up that treacherous grade even in four-wheel low.

We had to use our hiking poles just to keep our balance as the loose gravel made every step a challenge. Barney slid continually, and we each took turns falling down, until we learned to walk in the grass on the road edge. We could see why the state had such a monstrous steel gate. We have to admit, that had the gate been open, we likely would have tried, but that may have been disastrous! Neither of us had ever seen so many switchbacks, twists and turns, but we could see many of the signs of early logging, which would most likely have been done with horses and mules.

We finally saw that almost totally obscured place where, as you had noted in your book, that you hadn't taken time to investigate, because of your goal to reach the Whisky Creek Cabin, but we had been there so many times before from the river route, this hidden clearing was of more interest to us. There was at one time a very wide and well graded road going into that clearing, and once we were through the thick grasses, the forest above us shaded the road, so it was easy to walk and it was level.

The old road was quite easy to make time on, and in a short while we emerged into a fairly large, open field, that was full of tall grasses and brush of all sorts; the kind that promises to tear one's clothing and make you sorry you intruded. After another ten minutes of wandering around, we found an old corrugated metal shed with a door hanging by only one twisted bracket, so of course, we had to inspect it.

Barney went first, and with a bit of kicking at the ancient door, we finally had enough of an opening to squeeze through; after carefully scanning the inside with our key-chain flashlights. Outside of a bunch of old bolts and oil cans, there were a couple of rotting wooden boxes and upon closer inspection, we saw a neatly stacked double row of dynamite sticks.

Barneys' father had been a "hobby miner," so Barney showed me a sort of glistening area on a few of the sticks; which he said was nitroglycerin, and before he could tell me more, I was once again, back outside in the field!

There didn't appear to be anything else of interest, as we

retraced our path back, but a disturbance on our right, way down at the far end of the field caught our attention. There in the area of a huge mountain oak tree, a bunch of crows had suddenly gathered, and they were furiously scolding some poor victim of their rath. Naturally, we had to investigate further, as there must have been over twenty of the frenzied characters and more on the way. Picking our way through the growth of brush, and avoiding the dangerous raspberry bushes, we drew rapidly closer, until we were within about twenty-five yards of the commotion when we spotted two more of those corrugated metal sheds. The crows seemed to be stirred up at something right ahead of us, so we cautiously crept forward until the only thing between us and those open sheds were a bunch of shorter willow bushes. Barney had drawn his revolver a while before, as a precaution, and I now saw him gesture to it as a signal to draw mine as well. Although we had never had any close calls, one never knows what kind of danger you may be faced with, and I now had my gun in hand; pointing down with my forefinger on the trigger guard.

Suddenly there was a horribly loud screech, that was reminiscent of a mountain lion's scream, which once you've heard it, you never wish to again! Before I could even recover; there, not thirty feet away, with a loud sort of shriek, stood a huge Sasquatch! The beast had to have stood nine feet tall, which at the time seemed like twenty. Over its left shoulder, was slung a large blacktail female deer, and in its right paw was a large rock, almost bowling ball size; which it hurled at the excited audience with such force that it smashed through the treetops scattering branches and crows in all directions! We had been frozen in place, as everything seemed to be standing still, and only then did the monster turn in our direction, and for a moment, its reddish-yellow eyes seemed to widen, and we didn't dare move, but fortunately for us, the monster, had no intention of socializing, and in a couple of quick, long bounds he was gone!

That was for us, the single most exciting experience we have ever had, because this was the closest, we have ever been to the bigfoot creature and really what we consider, "up close and very personal!"

Everything after that was pretty much mundane, as we completed the long winding way to the Whisky Creek Cabin and there were quite a few rafters and a few river trail hikers there, but we created quite a stir when we came hiking down the hill from among the trees! Some of these people had been there awhile, having a picnic, and of course, no one knew there was even a road there.

We didn't plan to reveal our adventure, but when a couple from Grants Pass asked jokingly, if we had seen any Sasquatch, it was too hard for me to resist! By the time we finished sharing our experience; all mouths were gaping; and when the whole audience insisted on going up the mountain, we had to refuse, and we explained that we were doing so, not only for the Sasquatch, but for their safety as well. I once, again reiterated my perception of this snarling giant, and when one of our audience pointed out the handguns on our belts, they seemed to more readily accept the fact that even armed as we were; we had been afraid to even move.

*Whisky Creek Cabin was built about 1880 by an unknown gold prospector.*

It turned out that the couple from Grants Pass, owned a consignment store that we had done a lot of business with; selling items we no longer wanted, and they had previously seen several Sasquatch, but always far off, while they were rafting on the Rogue River.

Our return trip was gut-wrenching, and exhausting. Somehow, the way back seemed twice a far as when we came down.

We had forgotten, just how many switchbacks there were, and around each of the last six or seven corners, Barney swore the gate just had to be there! As for myself, I also felt that it would have to be there soon, as both of our water bottles were down to drops and I kept having visions of the cooler in our car! Then, finally, when we had stopped to rest for the umpteenth time, we saw the gate. Then it still took another ten minutes to stagger to the car.

After that harrowing experience last year, we are anxiously waiting for the incessant spring rains to cease, so we may once again make the trip back to that same place, but this time with larger packs and sleeping bags, and a camera. Stand by for what we hope will be another report; hopefully with Sasquatch photos!

*Publisher's note: The story of this couple's adventure was verified a while after we received this submission by a local ranger who was assigned to that area, and we were told that all of that aging dynamite has been destroyed. Thanks to these nice people from all of us!*

# OREGON CAVES BIGFOOT

By Helen S.

My name is Helen, and my husband Tim and I both grew up in San Diego, California, where we met at the Department of the U.S. Navy; where we still work after all these years.

Our annual vacations have taken us to many states, and after so many years, we finally decided to visit to visit our neighboring state, Oregon. We felt that, for once, we would have a leisurely time, instead of rushing to see everything of interest, and to sort of relax more and drive, less.

Our plan called for a direct trip to Portland, and a leisurely return by way of Highway 101 that runs from Canada to Mexico. With a constant, oceanside view all the way home, and stopping frequently to sightsee, it would be a totally relaxing vacation for a change!

All of our planning went right out the window the first night in Oregon, however! We stopped in Grants Pass, Oregon on our way to Portland, and were relaxing in the lounge of our motel's restaurant after an enjoyable dinner.

We couldn't help but overhear the two couples' conversation at the next table; who were totally engrossed in discussion about a creature that we had heard about for all our lives, but had always assumed it to be just a gimmick to keep us Californians out of Oregon. This conversation however; was between two couples living in Southern Oregon, and not in any way intended for our ears.

The two couples seemed to be so totally immersed in discussion, that their server had to interrupt them to take their drink order. That was when they must have noticed our presence, and we felt obliged to apologize for intentionally eavesdropping, but we were fascinated, and we both told them so.

Suddenly we found ourselves with the waiter's assistance, joining our two tables, and after introductions all around, we felt compelled to politely question whether their intent was to "toy" with one another, or if this Sasquatch could possibly be real. After only a few minutes, we were "old friends!" It turned out that one couple owned a retail store in Grants Pass, while the other couple was involved in a jet boat company on the famous Rogue River.

We were absolutely enthralled with their many experiences and sightings of this monster that we never before realized to actually exist! Enough so that the next morning we made calls to cancel reservations in Portland; and decided to instead, vacation totally in Southern Oregon.

We weighed the long hours on the freeway to Portland, and the very slow trip down the coastal two-lane highway fighting the boredom of bumper-to-bumper traffic with only the same ocean view, where even the ship traffic was over the horizon, so you couldn't see anything but the water.

We therefore instantly traded two weeks of fighting traffic, for a chance to relax and explore the possibility of perhaps seeing one of those Sasquatch/Bigfoot creatures!

We checked out early and after breakfast rolls and coffee, we headed toward our new reservations in the Oregon city of Cave Junction. Cave Junction is the only direct connection with the Oregon Caves National Monument, and it connects Interstate Highway 5 with the coastal highway 101.

So we checked in early, as we wanted to begin our Bigfoot research as soon as possible. For a small city, we were amazed at the number of vehicles everywhere we looked, and we saw license plates from states all across the U.S., Canada, and even one from Mexico.

The fact that school was still in session, was even more surprising to see so many tourists this early in the year. We began driving around the town looking for any place to park when we lucked out as a car pulled out of a curbside spot just ahead of us, and Tim was instantly at the curb!

As we exited our car, and began to scope out the stores, right up the block was one of those; "Must Visit" places, carrying the name, "Bigfoot Print and Copy." How could we resist, since our world was now preoccupied with thoughts of this creature?

One would have thought that they were serving free drinks in the back room, at the amount of traffic, crowded into this small area, and our hopes for a casual conversation with the owner were soon dashed, but we did find several books on the Sasquatch, and purchased a copy of each one, and got out of the claustrophobic atmosphere with every intention to return later.

Incidentally those books were all published by "Swanson Publishing," so that is how we came to sending you our own experience if you wish to use it. {"Thanks for the plug! The Swansons."}

We had lunch and proceeded to check-in, and we made a quick trip to stock the small fridge in our room, and returned to immerse ourselves in studying your collections of others who had experiences with these animals so we could maybe learn from them. Had we not done this research; we may never have had the enjoyment that we did.

While in Oregon, we were pleasantly surprised by the friendliness of the people, because we had always heard that Oregonians were hostile toward Californians. Maybe they only act that way if we were planning to move there?

The next day, we headed for the Oregon Caves National Monument and spent the entire day there. First a cave tour, which made us glad to have brought jackets, and we visited the beautifully constructed Chateau which was undergoing restoration. An elderly visitor told us his father had worked on the original structure back in the 1920's.

When our cave tour was assembling, I guess I started a sort of chain reaction, when in conversation with a local area resident, I asked her if she had ever seen a Sasquatch. By the sudden reaction, one would have thought I passed gas or something as heads snapped around, and a dozen people were silently waiting for her response!

The poor ranger had her hands full, as the lady answered in the affirmative; but the quick-thinking guide interrupted us with a sharp chirp of her whistle, and we were off to the cave. As we walked, the lady quietly indicated to me that the creatures were definitely plentiful in the area, but we were separated in the group before she could elaborate further.

*Most every bit of material used to construct the Chateau at the Oregon Caves is native to Oregon. From the cedar bark on the outside to, the massive double fireplace of marble carved from a nearby hillside.*

Several people that had heard my query came over when the very enjoyable tour ended, and several of them seemed very anxious to share their personal experiences with Bigfoot. While we would have liked to hear more, and with the facility closing, they were ushering everyone out, as there were no overnight guests, they closed early. Ordinarily, we were told, when the hotel was open you needed reservations a year in advance.

We returned the following day to hike some of the trails that seemed to be really fun, and would give us a feel for the country. People we met while hiking all seemed to at some point or another to bring up the bigfoot subject, and we then understood that it was the policy of the staff to avoid the reference to the creatures, but it seemed to be everyone's wish to see a Sasquatch.

I saw a man whose face looked familiar, and he was angling directly toward us, and I recognized him as one of the staff that had avoided answering the Sasquatch questions the day before. As he drew within a few feet, he surprised us by saying; to Tim, "I see that you've travelled." This was in reference to the Masonic ring Tim was wearing, and was a code between the brotherhood of those in the Masonic Lodge. Knowing their code word, I relaxed then as the two men exchanged their ritual handshake that verified their brotherhood, and the bond of total trust was formed!

We accepted the invitation from Tim's new "brother" to join him for lunch, and we enjoyed a pleasant meal in a rather private corner of the dining room that seemed to be set aside from regular access by guests, and we enjoyed a half hour's dissertation that left us with no doubt that the Sasquatch was real!

Having formed such a bond between these men, when our new friend Taylor's wife Esther, suddenly joined us at the table, the four of us became instant friends! We came to find out that this couple had retired to this area eight years before, and had spent their careers in San Francisco, so they were overjoyed to find this climate so similar to home!

When they found out that we were nearing our own retirement, they invited us to their home the following Saturday; which we happily accepted. After spending the next few days travelling the back roads, and another hiking trip at the Caves, we arrived at the large gate at our friends' property.

The massive gate swung slowly open, and we entered under a huge rack of elk horns, and with the gate closing behind us, we saw a ranch house that Roy Rogers and Dale Evans would have been proud to own. As we pulled up in the driveway, Taylor was gesturing to a parking area in the shade of a massive oak tree. Their home was elegantly, but comfortably furnished, and after some refreshments, they invited us out on their spacious patio where we were surrounded by flowering trees of various types.

Being as how we had heard that they got a lot of rain, I brought up the subject to which Esther replied that; "the rain comes often, but it's always', a warm rain." We laughed at that, but Taylor gave us a wink.

We had a very enjoyable visit, and when we explained how we had come to change our entire planned vacation due to hearing about the Sasquatch that first night; their eyes met, and they both chuckled! We, of course, already knew that they believed the animals were real, so why did they react in that manner?

We were soon to find out; Esther invited us to see more of their property, so we happily followed them as they walked slowly down the well-worn dirt pathway, and they cautioned us to be as silent as possible, and talk barely above a whisper, with the hope of seeing one of their resident elk. We couldn't see over fifty yards ahead, as the trail was curving gradually to our right, around a tall hedge of some sort of an evergreen bush, and we were now surrounded by them on both sides.

Then, Taylor held out his hand for us to come to a stop, and he slowly waved us forward so Tim and I were in the lead. Directly ahead, the trail headed straight toward a dark, wide, tree covered valley and the mountains in the background still were holding on to their snow caps, but a sudden movement on the low hill just ahead of us caught my attention. There, not two hundred feet away, was not the elk I had anticipated, but we were that close to a Sasquatch! Tim must have seen it at the same moment, because he let out an audible gasp. Not enough to alert the huge animals though, so there we all stood. Staring open-mouthed, I whispered to our hosts, asking if they knew the animals would be there? Esther replied that they were pretty sure they would be, as the family of Sasquatch normally visited those apple and peach trees on a regular morning run.

There were two large animals, and two small ones, which our hosts said was unusual; with most of the Sasquatch they had seen over the years, they only had one offspring every two or three years. They attributed this smaller of the two, to the last few years of the widening variety of crops they had planted, to assure the animals of an adequate supply of food. Evidently, they only had young if the food was sufficient enough.

Later, they explained that they seldom planted much for themselves, but the fruits, nuts, corn, lettuce and even potatoes, were all for their "critters", as they referred to them.

We watched for a while, until the Daddy Sasquatch suddenly stood straight up, and appeared to be sniffing the air, and

Taylor whispered for us to back up, which we quickly did, and then we headed back to the house.

Our hosts explained that they often noticed the Sasquatch looking back at them, and generally, they continued their harvesting without running away, however this time with four of us in view, they thought it best to retreat, and we were respectful of that, and ever so grateful for the once in a lifetime experience!

Returning home was a thought-provoking trip that was filled with the now exciting thoughts that our retirements were only five and seven years away, and we planned to keep in touch with Taylor and Esther, and think hard about the offer they made to sell us forty acres contingent to their land, if we chose to move there! I can truly say that unless these memories fade away for some reason, we may just end up planting gardens for a Sasquatch family of our own!

# OK, CONVINCE ME

By Tara Jenkins

Moving to this place on the Columbia River in Washington seemed like I had left all civilization! Moving here to begin with was a huge decision! I had made an agreement with my husband Ruben, that I would give it one year, and he had written and signed the contract that stated: "If after one year, Tara is not completely happy with living here, we will move to a state of her choosing."

Since we married thirty-two years ago, I had long been away from my birthplace in Virginia, and I had rather enjoyed our home in Seattle where we were both employed in the aircraft manufacturing industry. We had retired there, but Rube had always had the desire to return to his "roots." He had been born and raised in a small town; The Dalles, Oregon, and he kept trying to talk me into looking at moving anywhere near there.

My having a retirement clause in a large investment that would cost me a penalty if I left the State of Washington, we agreed to a compromise and looked for a rural property on the Washington side of the Columbia River, and we lucked out in finding a newer home with acreage that the seller agreed to allow us to rent for a year with option to purchase at an exceptional price. His wife said she was sick of the rain, while we had become so used to it, so we grabbed the opportunity!

The home is a mile or so, from the Columbia River, and the

house sat atop a rather large hill from which we could see the Columbia River, and we have a superb view of Oregon's, Mount Hood from our large deck! I had to admit that it was strikingly beautiful, but I was afraid of being so remote. Vancouver, Washington and Portland, Oregon were only an hour or so away, which brought about my agreeing to the deal, as civilization was at least close.

We made the move, and I'll have to admit that the steam whistle from a passing ship gave me a fond memory of my childhood home. After we had settled in, and made a few shopping trips to the Portland malls, I was ready to be "sold," so I told Rube to "start selling!"

We were soon carrying backpacks and heading out into the National forest that bordered our property line, and we found that the beautiful forests were absolutely crisscrossed with hundreds of deer and elk trails! Since much of this area was a designated Wilderness Area, we had no intention in doing any shooting, but the handguns we carried were at the advice of the local rangers.

When it came to the subject of Sasquatch, I'll admit to being highly skeptical, and Ruben had long ago ceased trying to convince me of their existence, but I had never bought into it. Now, however, when we had visited the local rangers the subject had come up purely by accident, even though at first, I thought Rube had asked them to stage it for my benefit.

A young couple were telling the rangers that they had been chased by Bigfoot, and they seemed sincere enough, but I was still suspicious until it was our turn at the counter. The ranger never even mentioned the creatures, and my curiosity forced me to address it.

The man politely asked that if and when we should encounter one, to please quickly back away, and not even attempt to approach it, as they were very docile until they sense danger, and then he said, "They think they're King Kong!" That was enough for me, and as I had so easily accepted this as the truth, I wondered why I had never before taken it seriously?

We began making regular explorations into our property and gradually stretching out into different areas of the government lands surrounding us until we had accumulated a collection of favorite routes throughout many miles of territory, and in all of those many miles, we had only once seen another human being.

Ruben showed me why it made sense, because after the main road arrived at our property, it turned away sharply and went around the rugged rocks that bordered our hill, and when it once again curved back around, the distance to return near our land was about ten miles through rough terrain. I realized then why so few vehicles ever came anywhere near us, except for forestry rigs.

On our explorations, we had seen large numbers of elk, blacktail deer, fox, coyotes, all types of squirrels, ravens, crows, hawks, eagles, and so many species, I could not even begin to list every one of them, but I reminded Rube that I still had never seen one of his "mythical Sasquatch." That must have triggered something in nature, because on our very next outing, I got my proof; in spades!

We began venturing deeper into the forests with each trip, and gradually learned the fastest routes through the massive forests. During our explorations, we came across an increasing number of wolf tracks, and according to the rangers, there should have been only a few remaining; however, we identified two distinctly different, very large prints, and with the differences in the rest of the packs' prints, there had to be two separate families of these wolves! There definitely was a sizeable difference in the two adults in each of these packs. The coyotes were less than the rangers had suspicioned, but we felt it had to be because of the numbers of wolves.

I was personally more afraid of the large cougar tracks, and one day when we ended up returning by our same route, we saw fresh tracks where a cougar had followed us! Finding cougar prints over our own tracks made only hours before was unnerving to say the least, and I found my hand reaching back often to feel the reassuring grip of my handgun.

Once we came upon a cougar with a deer that it had recently killed, and instead of retreating, it just stood over the deer and snarled at us! The animals' teeth were enough to give me nightmares, and its snarl gave us all the reason in the world to back straight away. That blood curdling scream echoing through the forest was further evidence that the cougar did not wish to be disturbed any further!

I experienced a rude awakening at that point, because I had always heard that all wild animals in our state automatically yielded their space before humans, but they must have forgotten to notify the cougars! We also saw a few bobcats, but they never remained in view for more than a few seconds before they disappeared.

As we backed away, I noticed the revolver in Rubens' hand, and I was reassured in my suspicions that the cougar was not about to back away. Perhaps it had little mouths to feed. Realizing that it was no different than someone approaching me when I was loading groceries in the car at Walmart, I too, would be alarmed and defensive. After all, we were interrupting the cougar's shopping trip and its meal.

The early spring gave way to a beautiful summer; the small accumulation of snow was soon gone, and we were anxious to resume our exploring, and Ruben was still selling me on the property that he had very obviously fallen in love with. I remained passive, relishing in Rubes' efforts to point out all of the plusses for going ahead with purchasing this property.

I, on the other hand, was still thinking that there were other more civilized places to live in this state.

*At one entrance to Ape Cave, on the southern slope of Mt. St. Helens, Washington State, USA. The cave is a lava tube beneath ground surface and entrances are created when ground above tube collapses.*
*By: Tequask / CC BY-SA (https://creativecommons.org/licenses/by-sa/4.0)*

Our next adventure was one that we had both looked forward to, but put off due to the early snowfall last year that would have caught us at too high an elevation to be safe, so now we were headed for "Ape Caves". I believe that it got its name from Gifford Pinchot who was president Theodore Roosevelts' Secretary of the Interior, and was also the presidents' brother-in-law, if my memory serves me right. Not that it matters, but it impressed me that such famous people were knowledgeable about this very spot.

We had carefully planned this trip for a year, and all of our research indicated that the first visitors to this area were assaulted by huge "apes" that pelted them with stones and rolled large boulders down on them from the cliffs above. We certainly weren't afraid of any ape people still guarding the caves; however, the rangers cautioned us that there may have been a group of Sasquatch way back then, before anyone had ever heard about their existence, and they very easily could have descendants that exist to this very day! We appreciated their words of caution, and the very real chance that there could be descendants of those mysterious apes, as the head ranger advised us, the attacks by apes had never been proven beyond a reasonable doubt, nor had they been disproven.

Spring gradually gave way for our first forecast for clear weather ahead, so having been befriended by a ranger whom we allowed to have access to a large pond on our property for an experimental trout study, he had accumulated a collection of old documents that all had individual reports from those who had documented their sightings and encounters, since the very first sighting.

He had been kind enough to make photo copies of them all, and he surprised us at our car, saying to please never reveal how we got them, and to please not share them with anyone. We knew he was taking a risk doing this, as the official policy of the department is one of total denial of the existence of any such creatures.

So, here we were on our second day in the darkness of the thickly forested valley, and the day was beautiful; with that early morning chill languishing in the small meadow as we ate a cold breakfast, and washed up in the ever-so cold stream that crisscrossed throughout this forest of heavy ground moss, scraggly spruce, and thick balsam trees.

The trail was easy to follow thanks to our ranger friend having hand-drawn a shortcut that we would likely never have found, and we would have run up against a steep cliff that the map did not indicate. Had we gone the way shown on the map we had previously purchased, we would have missed the place we now were walking through, and having wasted so much time, we agreed that we would probably never have tried again. What a loss that would have been!

Our ranger friend had told us that their department had always known of this error, but he admitted to the fact that they all agreed to leave it as it was, as they had plenty of rescues to perform without expanding the area which would likely have tripled their workload!

According to the hand printed notation on our copied map, the pathway had been drawn in by hand, so we carefully wound our way around the trail, and according to the notations in ink, we had to be getting close. There was a notation in the text that one of their party had totally disappeared, and when searching the area, the group came upon a high ridge that was apparently formed by a volcanic explosion from one of the area mountains that had suddenly appeared as a new peak that just burst open, spewing molten lava over this entire area, and causing this resident ape family to flee for their lives. After the violent eruption, there remained an entire network of caves, left as the lava cut its way through the molten rock, and it flowed at a fast enough speed that it left a huge network of smooth-walled, tube-like caves throughout a wide area. It was in those caves that these Bigfoot creatures made their homes.

These stories, and rumors of wild apes persisted over the years, and these wild tales of apelike creatures served to be a catalyst for the government to post the entire area as unsafe and off-limits. Numerous sightings and frightening encounters were reported, and these reports fueled increasing visitors until the forestry people declared the entire area as being unsafe and off limits to everyone.

So, here we were; likely the first visitors to these caves for a long while, and as we placed our packs on a small ledge near the opening, we retrieved our flashlights and spare batteries, and after camouflaging our packs behind a large chunk of ceiling that had fallen, we entered the large cave directly off to the left side of the trail. Our eyes were fighting to adjust to the total darkness, and we gradually were able to walk more easily on the narrow center of the cave where eons of time had formed a flat area composed of the gradually deteriorating ceiling of the lava tube we were travelling through. That made enough of a flat surface for comfortable walking.

At one point, where we had decided it was late enough in the day to seek shelter for the night rather than return all the way to the entrance, we were discussing whether or not we could even keep from getting panicky, and since Ruben was in the lead (we took turns, using one light at a time to conserve batteries), he turned off his light. Rather than being in total darkness as we should have been, there seemed to be another light source coming from way up ahead.

Taking enough time for our eyes to adjust, there was adequate light by which to see our way, but the first time Rube stumbled over a small piece of rock, the conservation idea was out. We continued for what must have been several hundred feet more, and suddenly, there was a huge opening in the outer wall of the cave, through which we exited into the brilliant mid-day's sun.

We sat down on some boulders to give our eyes time to again adjust, and directly facing us, only thirty or so yards away, was another cave that from where we sat, looked like a continuation of our same tunnel. We reasoned finally, that we had been travelling through a volcanic lava tube that had run across the valley and gradually hardened to leave a long, winding tunnel that reminded me of a huge black garden hose winding across the open expanse of this valley, from where we were now on the outside of the tube, it was easy to envision.

The bright sky revealed that the open valley all around us was lush with vegetation, and tall Ponderosa pine trees grew across the area, and some were only yards away from where we were.

We enjoyed a light snack and the brilliant sky chased away the chill of the cave. We were contemplating a return to the tunnel to resume our exploring, as we sat silently while leaning back against the incline of the rough lava when suddenly, our world changed!

I suspect that we both had fallen asleep, in our comfortable rocky lounge, when my senses made me open my eyes; not because of any noise, but more of a feeling than anything else.

I was too relaxed to do more than open my eyes, thinking that I must subconsciously have awakened due to the loud screech of the hawk floating gracefully overhead, but my eyes detected a slight movement directly across from me. There, standing like a statue, not forty feet away, stood a creature that I recognized instantly to be a Sasquatch! I found it funny; that in my shocked state, my mind projected a picture of me saying; "Doctor Sasquatch I presume?"

I still remember that strange thought, but thankfully, I hadn't even dared to take a deep breath. The animal was only about five feet tall, with a slight slump to its' shoulders, and as we stared at each other, it cocked its' large head as if trying to discern what I was. Then a movement behind it caused me to sit straight up, as there, towering above the focus of my attention, was a monster! The adult seemed to almost touch the top of the opening, and all I could compare it with was the gorilla in the Portland Zoo, only this animal was much larger!

Rube was awake now, due to my gasp, but as he looked up, the adult must have sensed a threat, and the horrible screech it let out was, as Ruben later put it, "enough to cause instant baldness!"

We were both wide awake, and even though we carried guns we had never before, drawn them for fear, yet here we stood, ready to defend ourselves against a behemoth! That, we later agreed, wouldn't have likely even felt pain before it tore us to shreds. Then, in a blink, both animals were gone!

We stood there visibly shaking, as we had hoped to someday see a Sasquatch, but with both of us having serious doubts, we were only going through the motion in order to keep such a fascinating mystery alive. Our explorations were now cut short, as neither of us had any desire for further explorations of the remainder of this lava tube, with what we knew was ahead of us somewhere in the dark tube!

We retraced our path out of the cave, and walked at a much faster pace, without realizing it, until we came across our previous night's camp, and it was only mid-day. We had not travelled all that far, but since we were both in a state of exhaustion, we made an early camp. Without speaking, we were each alone with our thoughts when I noticed Rube had withdrawn the roll of heavy twine that we carried for emergency wrapping for splints and such, and he was stringing the twine in a huge web all around the willows surrounding our campsite. Then, he retrieved an empty can from our trash bag, placed several small stones in it, and added the can to the string between branches. Testing several places in the network of his alarm system, Ruben, finally noticed me watching, and said, "custom Squatch detector." I know we both slept better that night!

Leaving at daybreak the next morning involved adding the alarm system to our carry-out trash collection, and a hasty breakfast. We made record time on our return, without the constant inspection of tracks on the trail, and we arrived home during dusk. Closing the door behind us was a great relief, and Rube said; it made his butt pucker.

Several statements that Ruben had made on our return trip, were an obvious attempt at, "taking my temperature" as I could tell that he feared our Sasquatch encounter may have swayed me against going through with purchasing this home; so at lunch on the patio, I calmly suggested that perhaps we should plant some apple, and pear trees, and a few Christmas trees for our later use.

You could see the smile on his face all the way from Seattle!

# MEETING MY SASQUATCH NEIGHBOR

## By David Young

Every time I take off for my favorite hike in the back of my extensive property, I seem to notice certain subtle changes in the scenery; especially when the Bigfoot creatures are about.

This was in my mind as I took my familiar route that led from that public campground bordering my property, down along the river, and through that slot canyon that came in from the right side near the bottom of that treacherously steep slope. I had traveled this area quite often after my two months of in and out of the hospital recovering from Malaria! I should say, learning to live with the fact that it can reoccur at any time, gives me an insecure feeling.

I contracted malaria on my last and final trip to South America on a Mission for my church and the completion of my service of two years of humanitarian efforts that had been quite successful; so I took great pleasure at having been of help. After my final devotion to service for the Lord, I now was looking forward to total relaxation.

My sister had watched over my home and property during my absences over these last years, and I was more than grateful for her diligence in having the gardeners maintain my lands, and even making sure my old Jeep had a full tank of fuel and a charge in the battery.

I was now ready to embark on a goal I had set when I purchased this place from my father's brother a few years back, after he had lived there for thirty years. Uncle Freddy had been injured at the mill where he had worked for most of his adult life, and took an early retirement on the generous insurance settlement; and since he had never married, he decided to spend his final years in a local retirement home where he had several friends who had kept urging him to join them.

My father had suggested that I purchase the property when I was myself retiring, and Uncle Freddy was more than generous in his price; saying he was glad to keep the place in the family, so he could still visit me on occasion; to which I gladly concurred.

My own wife had taken ill on our last mission for the church, and she had unfortunately passed away while I was still hallucinating in my Malarial stupor. It had been a terrible last two years; so now, all I wanted was to be alone with my memories and my two newly acquired dogs; Mutt and Jeff, who I named after an ancient comic book that I had found when cleaning out the attic when I moved in. The names seemed to fit my furry companions.

My "ranch," as I chose to call it, is not too remote, but the county road ends just past my property with a wide turn around, so most everyone knows that there is little sense to further drive it unless to see me, and that seldom ever happens. Even the traveling salesmen quickly learned the meaning of no.

The home just before mine belongs to an elderly couple

whom I will occasionally wave to on my trips to and fro, but we still have never met, and that seems to work for us. The snow plow and the mailman are about the only visitors; which suits me fine.

I think I had lived here about a year when I saw my first Bigfoot! I knew instantly what it was, because my father had told me way back to ask Uncle Freddy about his "freeloading sharecroppers." Uncle Freddy had seemed rather stand-offish about my request, and it took him a few minutes before he replied. He said, "Tell your old man to stay out of it!" Then after a minute, he realized that if I were to live here, it was only fair that I should know.

His demeanor suddenly changed then, and he began by telling me that there were just a few of these animals living in the forests behind my property, and then Freddy couldn't hold back any longer and he filled me in on what his secret was. Had I not grown up hearing stories about these Bigfoot animals, I would have thought he was crazy, and even though the stories were rampant in this area, I had never personally seen one. Uncle Freddy explained that I was likely to never even see one, as the small family of them lived far back in the canyon that began at the far edge of my property, and to even get there was a chore.

Uncle Freddy went on to tell me that years before, when the federal government closed off the entire area adjacent to my back-property line, they had totally bulldozed the entrance to that section of the canyon, as there had been too many emergency calls to rescue the four wheelers who "bit off more than they could chew!" The park's budget being cut, he told Freddy they had fewer resources for rescuing "idiots."

Although having never seen one of these Sasquatch, I also had never seen the "Boogy Man" either, but when I was a kid, I believed he was real, and that had never been disproven either.

While Freddy was explaining all of this to me, I thought back to those days in my youth to the old men sitting around that big wood stove at Dawson's General Store, who told stories of Bigfoot, so why would I even dare to doubt the word of my own father's brother?

Freddy hadn't made a big deal out of it, so I gave him my word that I would keep planting the potatoes, and that I would care for the apples and peaches that he said he raised strictly for his "friends." Since he told me flat out that this was the only "condition" of the sale, I readily agreed. He had one more add-on to my commitment, and that was that I would do my utmost to protect these Sasquatch, because they were just another of God's creatures that needed our protection to survive. Although still somewhat skeptical, I agreed.

Anyway, after all of my travels, I was home to stay, and I could finally see the property that I had never even been more than a few hundred feet out in. As I mentioned before, I was indebted to my sister for periodically hiring yard maintenance people and her occasional visits to check on everything in all of my frequent duties, and I now could finally relax.

Sis had been curious about why I wanted the fruit trees maintained, and who it was that kept constantly harvesting it, but when I just said, "friends," she gave me a knowing grin, and the gleam in her eyes told me that she knew about "them." I reasoned that she may have only been testing me.

So now, with a couple of good-sized water carriers and some snacks of sorts for myself, Mutt and Jeff, I buckled on my revolver and shell belt, and we were out the back door to our own private corner of the National Park, where even the rangers have likely never set foot upon.

In all the short trips I have made in this area, only one time did I ever see another human, and that was a lone hiker on a ridge far away. This very remote corner is twenty-four miles from the secondary entrance to the park, with only one small toilet, so most all visitors use the main entrance that is yet another twenty miles in the opposite direction. With budgets being constantly cut, it is in the rangers' best interests to concentrate visitors closer to where they can control and monitor the flow. Another factor to discourage visitors to my end is that overnight camping is prohibited in the entire region.

Uncle Freddy had told me that the Bigfoot family moved in shortly after the government had restricted this area from further services and they were not great in numbers, but after living here awhile, and knowing they were safe, he began seeing more signs of them, and they no longer were walking so as to intentionally avoid leaving a trail.

With tourists swarming all over the forests searching for them, who would even guess that a family of these creatures would be living so near a home and being nourished by their own private produce orchard and potato patch?

The dogs and I were soon enveloped in the massive forest

area that stretched for so many miles in this remote corner that I had never before been so far in, and there was nothing familiar after we had traveled for several miles. The area was rapidly descending into the ever-widening canyon, and as I glanced around at short intervals so as not to not lose my footing on the rocky areas where the ground was covered by various sizes of rock laid bare by the spring runoff.

Seemingly, out of the cliff itself, a rivulet of clear water suddenly began running alongside the trail which caused us to more carefully watch where we stepped. This stream grew wider until we finally arrived in a beautiful canyon stretching to our left and right, and our stream had made a gradual curve to the right and was joined by another stream coming in from our left; the water was now about two feet wide and the crystal-clear runoff was now about a foot or two deep. The canyon's walls were now gradually narrowing, and the descent had steepened to where we had to constantly be aware of every step in the constantly narrowing walls. There was little vegetation, and what there was seemed to be made up primarily of sagebrush and various sorts of gnarly bushes that were literally covered with thorns that threatened to rip flesh and clothing to shreds, and the dogs knew to steer clear, and that kept me safe as well.

I had expected to see grasses growing alongside the stream, but judging from its obvious snakelike course, the water seemed to wander through ever-changing routes; which I related to the frequent thunderstorms that often visited this area. As the canyon began to level off, I could no longer see where we had made our decent, and everything behind us looked to be a constant repetition of the scenery up ahead.

I kept thinking if there was a quick rain that obliterated our tracks, that I should have marked our exit with some of the red flagging in my backpack. That thought gave me cause to tie a long flag on the nearby sage, and I also made a mental note of how long it had taken us to reach this spot, as I had checked my watch as we reached the bottom of this canyon.

My intention had been to try to relate how far we went in the same direction from which we had come from the house. Later on, I intended to see if there was a direct route from the house to the canyon without having to make this rectangular trip. Since this was such a strikingly beautiful place, perhaps I could find a short-cut. I found this remote area to be seemingly untouched by humans, which I'm certain was due to the fact that everywhere else in the park had more items of interest. And that suited me just fine.

I stopped finally to grab a snack, and give my "kids" a couple of treats, and since they seemed to prefer drinking repeatedly from the cold, clear steam, I didn't worry about rationing my water.

Another thing making this area so peaceful was that air traffic here was forbidden due to the area being a national Condor reserve. A nesting pair of the nearly extinct birds was known to be within the park boundaries, so that prevented private plane owners from scouting this entire area. That works for me!

As we traveled further in the canyon, another thought hit me; the very noticeable fact that there were no cigarette butts and no candy wrappers that normally accompany human occupied areas. How nice!

Now, the sand dunes were almost as hard as clay, due to the constant sun, and the walking was easier now as I barely was sinking in the hardened sand. The canyon had narrowed slightly, and the stream had gradually widened as it was continually being added to by small streams feeding into it. Vegetation was almost totally absent, and this was understandable, because the signs of frequent flash floods made it impossible for any vegetation to gain a foothold. The stream was deeper now, and ever widening as it headed rapidly to emerge into the rich agricultural areas fifty miles away. Here I was, able to step across the water that further downstream would become a raging torrent.

I was thinking about how wonderful it was to be totally away from human presence; when my daydreams were shattered by the monstrous footprint directly before where I was about to step. There was a very distinct print that had to have been made by a Sasquatch! I had been aware of certain depressions in the sand, but I supposed them to have been made by a large elk, but since the drifting sands had all but filled them in, I thought little about it. Now, however, it was different. This print had the very definite imprints of toes!

Thoughts raced through my mind wondering if this giant was close by, and if it would know that I was the one who constantly supplied it and its family with food, or if it would rip my head off instead?

The depressions near the stream were more prominent in the damp sand, and placing my foot in one of the prints, I could still see the large track all around the sole of my size eleven boot. That was sufficient to totally grab my attention, and Mutt and Jeff were snorting around the tracks as if the scent had lingered, and the hair on their backs was standing straight up. That, plus the fact that the water was faintly building in the print, told me it was very fresh!

They both began growling, and their lips started to curl slightly, but this is where I was glad that I had them professionally obedience trained, as they stayed right beside me. My hand automatically felt back to touch the security of the revolver on my belt, but from the size of those prints, I certainly didn't feel all that secure!

Then my mind pictured what I would feel if my holster had been empty? My retreat would have been instantaneous. I had long thought of what would happen if I ever really met a Sasquatch, but in my heart, I never really expected I would!

I did know that I would never shoot one, but beyond that, I never thought any further, as it had been hard for me to even accept their existence, let alone what I would do if I ever met one.

The way ahead was rapidly narrowing, as the gorge curved slightly to our left, and now it seemed to be descending at a much steeper grade. The cliffs on each side were much closer together now, but I could see in the distance, that after passing through this narrow place, the canyon opened again to its prior width, and that helped me to relax a bit.

Now, as I stepped cautiously forward, my mind assaulted my senses with a vivid picture of this giant monster ripping my head clean-off and throwing it at my dogs! That mental picture gave me no desire to hurry in order that I may catch up to it, and I was perfectly content to set an even more leisurely pace. Mutt and Jeff were walking a bit faster, as I was sure they had no reservations about catching up, as they showed no fear, only the hair standing in ridges on their backs and the excitedly wagging of their tails and rapid turning to give me their anxious looks like; "Hurry up Dad!"

As I stumbled through the damp sand, I lost any concern about a face-to-face confrontation with this beast, as my only worry was to protect my overzealous dogs when they disappeared over a large dune, and I desperately lunged forward in my exhausted state, wishing belatedly that I had leashed them back up, because they paid no heed to my voice calls.

As I topped the dune, I sank to my knees at the top, too exhausted to go any further. I knelt there, gasping for breath, and way up ahead I caught movement in the sage growing abundantly on the far sloping wall of the canyon.

There, on the bottom of the steep slope stood my boys, staring up at the giant Sasquatch that was climbing up the wall; its huge feet sending waves of loose sand downward as it struggled toward the top.

My guys stayed at the bottom, staring up at the retreating beast that they no longer seemed to have any further interest in pursuing. A blast on my dog whistle was all it took, and they began trotting back to me, as if relieved to not be expected to attack the object of their pursuit.

I watched as the Sasquatch gained the top of the cliff, and it turned to look at me. It was really interesting, as there I was, watching this almost mythical animal, and I so-wished that I could communicate with it. Without even thinking, I subconsciously raised my right hand and gave a long, slow wave, as I would to a close friend. I felt embarrassed when I caught myself waving at this wild animal, however I was exhilarated when the huge creature returned my gesture with the same long, slow wave! Then it abruptly entered the forest and disappeared. The Sasquatch was long since gone when my boys were laying at my feet, tongues hanging out and taking turns lapping water from their collapsible bowl.

Well, time truly does fly, and it's been almost a year since our Bigfoot adventure, and the three of us are preparing for another excursion into Bigfoots' home, only this time, we go in style. I found an old map on which there is an ancient logging road that rounds through my property, and it shows where it intersects the canyon at about the same place as the Sasquatch was last in sight.

The boys and I are practicing our explorations with our new four-wheel drive, off road machine, and it even has a switch to run on battery only, so we can soon be sneaking in the back way to see that Sasquatch. This time though, we're bringing gifts from our orchard.

# JAPANESE GLASS FLOATS FOR SASQUATCH

By Jason Z.

Competing with a Sasquatch for a prized Japanese glass fishing float was the last thing I would have been concerned with on this cold and blustery day on the Oregon coast.

This was the time of year that I wrapped up in my warmest rain gear, and patrolled the pacific coast for those rare and beautiful floats that had broken away from the Japanese fishermen; many of which had floated the Pacific Ocean for years and years while the changing currents and vicious winds caused gigantic waves to keep these beautiful prizes at sea. Some, had been said to have floated out in the vast Pacific for up to forty-odd years, where the constantly changing weather patterns kept them floating aimlessly until finally plunging ashore on Oregon's sparsely populated Southern shores, and here I was, to welcome them to America.

This had become my hobby, since I chose this wild, and windy place to retire. I had been a commercial fisherman, and spent the better part of my career in supplying fish and lobster to the many canneries where I and my small crew became a regular supplier for the west coast restaurants and catered to many of the fanciest seafood tourist attractions.

This particular day was cold and blustery as usual, but the

winds were blowing harder than normal, giving the appearance of large panes of glass as they flashed in the shafts of brilliant sunshine that dared peek through the cloudy sky. I particularly enjoyed going out on these types of days, because the temperament of most beachcombers was such that they would be staying indoors. Only the most hardy souls would endeavor to ply their trade in such inclement weather, and knowing that had helped me succeed in this hobby of slowly diminishing returns

I had been very successful in finding these floats under the most dire circumstances, and I learned long before that the secret of successful beachcombing was to be there when even Mother Nature had stayed home.

Walking the shoreline at an extreme, forward angle was hard on the body, and the force of the constant wind seemed destined to blow a person apart, yet this was what one had to fight in order to succeed. Even native Oregonians soon tired of the long, fruitless searches that most often yielded only dead and dying sea urchins and sand dollars.

One lucky day, I found a beautiful, light blue float the size of a basketball, and this was highly unusual, so I carefully placed it in my large canvas retrieval bag and headed home. My uncle owns a tourist attraction on the Oregon Coast, and there in Brookings, Oregon, this particular prize should bring a huge amount; with its size and color being so rare.

All in all, I really enjoy finding these prizes, but this one particular morning after three days of unusually violent storms, I was again, out early and walking my usual distance from the surf, so I could alternately scan the distant sand dunes, as well as the surf. I saw in the distance what appeared to be a small child out in the surf, and he appeared to have retrieved a large glass float by the brilliant reflection in the sun. Although at that distance, I couldn't be sure, but the size of that float seemed enormous.

Hurrying, now, I ran as fast as I could on the harder sand at the shoreline; I really was pumping for all I was worth, because a golden float of any size was one of those "one in a thousand" finds, and uppermost in my mind was the thought of offering the child a large sum of money for his prize. I could picture that golden float on display at my uncle's place with a record high price in it! I had two goals racing through my mind; first, to caution that lad about the danger of getting caught by a "sneaker" wave and being quickly sucked out to sea, and secondly to see if I could buy that golden globe, for cash money. I planned to offer a generous amount, suspecting that later, I may be accused of taking advantage of a minor, so I intended to pay well for it, which I assumed he would gladly accept.

As I drew closer, I was guessing the youngster to be about ten or twelve years of age, based on his strides toward the sand dunes, His fur coat was soaked from the furious wind that had grown stronger and sent waves crashing, so I angled my course to intercept the kid at the dry sand just ahead.

The kid caught sight of me when I was about a city block away, and I gave a friendly wave, as beachcombers do, but instead of returning my wave, he picked up speed as if he was afraid of me. Not intending to break off my approach without at least making an effort to try buying the float, I broke into a run and increased my angle to intercept his path while staying out of the loose sand; as I knew by then, only a boy could run so fast carrying that large a float, and I had almost caught up when the kid made it over the first dune; I veered off to follow the depressions of his tracks, and I crossed over the dune right on his heels.

Then, I leaped over the top, to land on the bottom when I came to an abrupt halt. There was my quarry, only fifteen feet away, standing, facing me. There stood the defiant youngster, staring back at me, and the reason it had obviously lost any fear it may have had, was towering over it!

I had heard many stories and read about Sasquatch in these coastal mountains, but no one ever told me they were this monstrous. This giant was between me and the rising sun, and I was having to stare up at it, and being within its shadow, I was able to see every detail of this apelike being, and I seemed rooted in place, like I had no ability to move!

I am still thankful to this day that the pair decided to break off the meeting, as it could easily have broken me into bits! I admit that I have never been as genuinely afraid at any time before or since, and the adrenalin I had built up chasing that prized float now burned away and left me totally exhausted. I was finally able to breathe again, when they quickly departed.

I struggled to stagger, and crawl to the top of that dune the pair had crossed, and I plopped down on it and sat watching as those animals quickly disappeared into the green and black of the thick forest that stretched as far as the eye could see to both north and south.

I had no camera with me of course, because nothing very interesting ever happens on my weekly hikes!

# SASQUATCH IS MY COUSIN

By Belinda "Bell" Moses

My recollections of our family's frequent visits to my grandparents' home bring back fond memories for me and my brother Darcy. Our family wasn't all that sociable, as both of our parents worked long hours. Father was a shop teacher at the school that housed grades one through twelve, and Mother worked three days a week at our county hospital on the edge of town.

During summers, Darcy and I were pretty much in Dad's care, as he only had a few sporadic special classes for adults. We were fortunate that Mother's parents were always eager to have us spend much of our summers with them, and they spoiled us rotten!

Since dad spent a lot of time fishing, and since Darcy and I hated to sit there and hope some poor, slimy and smelly fish would decide to bite on a poor worm, we were never invited anymore to witness creatures die. Sensitive; yes, but then maybe you aren't bothered by some poor fish laying in the bottom of a boat, gasping for air; we were!

Our Grandparents had lived in their same home for many years, and their nearest neighbor was two miles away, on this long, narrow dirt road. Mother always made reference to her birthplace as "living in the sticks," which I never understood until I grew up. Now I do.

The house was built atop a large hill, and the long, deeply rutted driveway usually had a lot of weeds growing in the middle that always seemed to be the same height. The water runoff from frequent rains kept the growth about the same height, and the vehicular traffic seemed to keep the center short. When the grasses grew too high, Grandfather brought out the weed trimmer and made short work of them.

The home sat on the crest of the knoll, and was the typical two-story farmhouse of the times, with the garage sitting about fifty feet back from the back door. Unlike homes today where the attached garage is the norm, in those days the people would park alongside the back door, and the family vehicle sat beside the house in all sorts of weather. The garage was generally the place for current projects and used to park during the mid-winter snowstorms, and then, only when convenient.

I guess Grandfather had elaborate plans; however, he had an accident shortly after moving there, and it kept him from ever following through on his plans. He was forced into retirement from that accident at the mill where he had been for all of his adult life, and fortunately for everyone, he received a generous monthly check, so the shop underneath the garage remained in a state of neglect, as if it wasn't of further use.

I was very close to Grandfather, as we always took long walks into what he called "the back forty". I guess that was in reference to the size of the thickly forested land. I think I remember Grandfather telling me that the place had started out to be a Christmas tree farm, but he had decided to just let it grow wild. I remember going along at Christmastime to help haul back Christmas trees with my dad and grandpa for our use only. The rest of the trees just continued to grow.

This beautiful, dark forest came to within a couple of hundred feet of the garage, so Darcy and I had our secret places, and "forts" throughout the fragrant trees.

I also remember that Grandfather never ventured very far from the house without his trusty revolver on his side, and there was a football field sized gravel pit that was owned by the county, but hadn't been used for as long as I can remember, and the road to it had been blocked years ago by a huge pile of concrete slabs and busted up pieces of concrete from a bridge demolition that the county had also deposited directly in front of the entrance, which served to remove all chances of anyone using the pit for target shooting and causing the usual mayhem with drinking and public nuisance complaints, as happen to ancient pits like this.

Everyone in the community seemed to have forgotten about the pit, and the county had even cut out the former entrance by removing the culvert and continuing the drainage ditch alongside the road, so that ended any public access.

Many years back Grandfather had used his small bulldozer to make a road back behind the first trees that went directly to that abandoned pit, and he let me drive the small dozer when I got older. I remember it was called a Clark Airborne, and Gramps told me it had been manufactured to drop from airplanes to build airstrips on pacific islands during World War Two. It wasn't much bigger than many garden tractors are today, but extremely heavy and very powerful.

When I think back to actually having driven that machine while Gramps sat beside me, I wondered if our secret road was still back there, and I vowed to see for myself. Using that road to reach what had now been assumed by the local people to be Grandfathers property, I vividly remember the day Gramps pulled out those small orange ear plugs, and helped me get them in my ears while protecting his own as well, and then I learned to shoot a handgun. That first shot almost caused that long barrel to hit my head, but I held tight, having already seen the violence of a .357 Magnum. Most of our target practice was with one of Grandfather's .22 caliber pistols, revolvers and rifles; and I enjoyed them a whole lot more.

Today, with Grandmother's permission, I once again went to the gun cabinet, brought out my own belt and holster, loaded my revolver, and with my hiking boots double knotted, and a canteen of water, and many grandmotherly cautions, I headed out back to walk through old memories!

I walked straight back toward the forest until I arrived at the road leading to the gravel pit, and turned right, but I only went a couple of hundred feet, and then I made a sharp turn to my left, and the old, but long-abandoned, power line clearing was still, after all these years only lightly overgrown with brush and weeds.

There were only a few young spruce trees that had been able to take root, due to the rocky shale that covered this part of the land. Walking on the convenient animal trail, my legs soon brought back painful memories of my following

Grandfather up this very path, taking two steps to his one, and after what seemed a half day, but was only an hour, I was within fifty feet of the top; and then; remembering our ritual, I cut sharply left and entered the thick, dark forest of closely growing balsam trees.

Like it was only yesterday, I instinctively followed the same animal trail that I remembered from all these years, and there it was. The gigantic, white boulder that was laden with streaks of marble and a sort of agate!

Climbing atop the behemoth was easier now as I was an adult, and within moments, I was sitting in the same place I had so many times in the past, and subconsciously I found myself brushing away the buildup of pine needles from Grandfather's place as well.

I sat there for the longest time in the haze of a flood of precious memories without even a thought of the present when I suddenly became aware that I was not alone. There, as if it had also come to share my childhood adventure; not sixty feet in front of me, my dreamy state pictured my remembrance of that day so long ago when I saw my very first Sasquatch!

I could feel a smile tugging at my face as I thought back to that exciting moment, when I was shocked out of my dream when the large animal suddenly cocked its large head, as if trying to see if I was real or in, its' own imagination. Although everything must have taken place in only a few seconds, it seemed like many minutes, before we were both aware of one another. Still, neither of us moved, other than our breathing seeming faster, and perhaps that magnificent creature had been one of those youngsters that Grandfather and I had so often watched play at their parents' feet while neither those adult Sasquatch, nor we, ever moved from our places.

I remember distinctly how Grandfather had prepared me for my first trip to visit his "friends," and how he had repeatedly gone back over everything that we were about to see until I finally agreed to not scream when I saw his imaginary friends, and I remember telling myself that I wanted to please Grandfather, so I made up my mind to pretend that I saw it also. I will never forget my absolute shock, accompanied by pleasure at finding that the Sasquatch were real, and Grandfather was sane!

Now, today, I was wishing that I also had someone to share this wonderful experience with. As a child, I never once betrayed the secret that we shared, and now that Grandfather was gone; whatever could I do? My parents had invited me back here to help convince Grandmother to move in with them in order to better care for her, and they planned to sell this home and property.

How my mind was racing now. I wished that there was some way to be able to tell them about how special this property really is, and how it holds more than pleasant memories; it also owes an obligation to carry on Grandfather's promise.

As I made my way back to the house, I walked slowly; contemplating my own circumstances, and since my divorce, I had settled into a very convenient condo, and being an independent contractor, my work found me traveling all over the country from my home in Aurora, Colorado, and I thought back to what Grandfather said on so many occasions when we had lunches atop that huge boulder where our Sasquatch friends so often shared our luncheons together; we with our sandwiches and they, enjoying their gifts of fruits and vegetables that we had packed along. Grandfather would always lean back on his favorite spot atop that huge boulder and say: "I can see Denver from here!"

My plans were formed by the time I returned to the house, and my parents had already arrived for supper, so the timing could not have been better. Knowing that my folks planned to invite Grandmother to live with them; she had assumed that this was coming, and expressed what my parents had already discussed many times; and that was the lifetime of memories that she would miss by leaving her home, yet she knew it was best for all concerned.

I waited until my folks had made her their proposal, and before Grandmother could respond, I joined the conversation with my offer to buy her property at fair market value. I reasoned that if it was mine, then in a way it would still be hers, and she was always welcome.

My condo sold the third day, and it has been three months now, and I have already made a half dozen trips up to what Grandfather often referred to as "The Lookout," and I have on the last two trips brought some work with me, and now I can really enjoy working from home.

Last week, Grandmother was out for a visit, and just out of the blue, she asked me how the Sasquatch were faring. That really blew me away. This kindly little lady had let Grandfather and me play our game all those years, and she told me she knew the whole time about our furry friends!

# DO SASQUATCH HIBERNATE?

By Ralph Dunsworth

This is a subject that remains to be proven, however, we believe we have solved this question, at least for our region.

My interest in this project began when I attended a seminar conducted by the well-accredited Doctor, Jeffrey Meldrum, who is a respected authority on the Sasquatch/Bigfoot creatures.

Myself and a few other retired teachers of varying subjects, all met over and during several different occasions while attending the most entertaining subject of the Bigfoot creatures, and we eventually formed a study group; more for our own entertainment than for any officially sanctioned research.

Our major concerns came about after we found enough believable evidence that the Sasquatch does exist, but no credible evidence had been offered as to whether or not the creature hibernates. Therefore, I took it on myself to volunteer to do what no one else in our group was crazy enough to dare. I soon found out why!

One of our team has a close friend, whom we will refer to as "Sam," who left the world of academia to retire on a very remote property in Colorado that was pretty much central to much of the information that our group had gathered regarding the majority of the most credible claims of Sasquatch encounters and sightings. Our contact was kind enough to secure an invitation for me to travel up into this remote location and use this man Sam's private road through his acreage to gain access to an otherwise impossible route to a mountain canyon that was often referred to as the "Sasquatch Ridge." In fact, our group is in possession of three old and out-of-print maps that all refer to the same "Sasquatch Ridge Trail."

Since my partner had such a close relationship with the man who we call Sam, we obtained permission to gain access to the almost inaccessible old road that we had seen referenced on the old government maps as "Sasquatch Ridge," and the thin dotted line leading to the ridge as "Sasquatch Ridge Trail."

Sam told us that the references to these animals were immediately removed before the next printing due to the fact that two, two-man teams, had totally disappeared over a six-month period, and both of their abandoned vehicles were found at the same trailhead that their teams had used for their mountain assent. No trace of the men was ever found! Thus, the authorities removed all reference to the Sasquatch.

There were only a few of the old cartographers around anymore that had any recollection of those bygone days according to Sam, and he allowed us to use his copy to make notations on our current production map, and my partner Roy noted in ink the thin line that led up as "Sasquatch Trail" and the horizontal bar indicating the ridge line as "Sasquatch Ridge;" there he made a star to mark our destination.

The only evidence those lost teams, was a silver-plated whisky flask that had the initials of a doctor of anthropology who was with one of the two teams, but not another shred of evidence was ever discovered; only their vehicle.

It had taken quite a bit of wrangling and finagling for our team members to get permission for us to use this man's property for my search, but he absolutely insisted that there be at least two of us to make the trek, and he also made us agree to leave another two men to make a base camp at the place the ancient road stops and the trail begins to ascend the canyon leading to the mesa far above.

We readily agreed, and then we had to go through selecting those four men who would go, as it now seemed that the entire group wanted to go. Out of respect for the use of Sam's property, we narrowed the selection to a final three plus myself, whom he concurred with.

We prepared as best we could, and from previous explorations that many of us had learned from, we made pretty short work of gathering our supplies, and since the first traces of the colors of Fall were already hitting the upper mountains, we were all set at base camp. Roy and myself, who would make the trek upward found ourselves shouldering our more than heavy backpacks and waving goodbye to our comrades below as we began the gut-wrenching ascent up the trail. Jerry and Bill were chopping firewood from an old log as we left, so they would be comfortable.

Thanks to Sam's generous permission to use this upper route, we were already a day or two closer to our goal of reaching what we perceived from our research, and visual sighting through our binoculars, to be a huge plateau atop where we were now headed. It wasn't long before we had to make our first stop, to rest our legs from the intense pain of the climb, and already the altitude was taking its toll on us both. Before too much further, the inch of the previous day's snow was making our climb even more difficult, as the light snowfall had covered the trail just enough to camouflage the loose rocks underneath. This slowed our progress considerably.

We continued to climb toward a rather dark, wide area beneath a snow-covered overhang, and it gave the appearance of a jutting cliff under which we might rest a bit from the light snow that had now begun to fall. The kind of flakes that seem to have a penchant for sticking to eyebrows and eyelashes, so one finds himself continually wiping them away as when fighting mosquitoes in a swamp. Not nearly as painful however.

Roy thought to take a compass bearing to check our path ahead with our map, however, there was some sort of magnetic attraction that eliminated any chance of accuracy. Besides that, I jokingly remined him that the only direction that we cared about was "up!"

As we rounded the gradual turn to our right, the trail almost seemed to be guiding us to a specific goal, as the climb was becoming easier and we were no longer having to step over rocks and boulders. A few hundred yards further, we found ourselves approaching a thick pine forest on a kind of mesa. Almost as if the entire top of this tall peak had suddenly been sheared off and a thick forest had mysteriously sprouted up. Even the trail we were now walking on was dirt rather than hard rock, and the dirt was thickly covered in pine needles.

We now seemed to be on a well-pronounced and well-traveled trail, as we wound slowly around the peak of this low mountain toward the strange shaped cone on top that we only had an occasional glimpse of up until now.

As the trail continued through the forest, I was still continually looking for what type of animals were using it, and the unnerving sight of a large and unmistakable paw print of a bear stopped me in my tracks, and Roy came up from behind me to see what I was kneeling over. We determined that it was a track of a black bear and not a grizzly, which if it had been a "grizz," I would have probably wanted to give up going further. The track was the only clear print, as it was in a sheltered dirt area where the snow had failed to cover it.

After Roy examined the track more closely, he determined from his extensive hunting experience that it was likely several days old, and he surmised that with the sudden change in the weather two days before, that the animal was likely in a den somewhere close by and we could forget about him until late spring.

I breathed another sigh of relief as the tracks led downhill toward a thick grove of pines and a jumble of a landslide that had long ago devastated an entire grove of pines; it looked like a huge pile of places for bears to hibernate within. The apparently heavily used trail slowly continued in a wide arc around the high peak staring down at us until we once again entered another thick growth of pines and firs.

The trail had now become hard to navigate and Roy wondered aloud at how difficult it must be for deer or bear to travel such a circuitous route, and then we just stopped and looked at each other; "Sasquatch!"

As we now even more slowly continued on the trail, we stopped often to survey the forest around us as the trail narrowed, and we could now once again feel the cold wind that indicated we had come full circle around the peak of this lower mountain, and before we could decide what to do next, a sudden movement down the trail leading into the thicker firs below us made our choice clear.

There, not forty yards from where we stood was clearly a young Sasquatch. We had both been focused on where the trail we were on went down the hill and into the thick green wall of trees at a point beside a monstrously tall fir tree, and at that very moment, a Sasquatch that we figured to be about six feet tall by the way its height showed it to be next to a branch of the tree it immediately retreated behind upon spotting us as we blustered and pointed like amateurs at it. After all, there are few professional Squatchers, if any.

We cautiously and carefully made jour way down the short but steep slope and stepped into the narrow opening between the monstrous fir and another one about half as big next to it, where we found ourselves among the true giants of this well concealed forest that almost totally blocked out the sun.

It was colder now, and we had used up almost all of our daylight in our excitement, and it was even more apparent in this dark but beautiful forest. We forgot all about the Sasquatch with night about to descend, and we fortunately found a large monolith of a fir that must have fallen from old age or fierce wind, as it lay with its trunk extending down the steep slope and we took shelter in the huge hole beneath the root ball that had long since lost its spidery roots. We gathered up the aging pieces of branches and limbs that had dried over the years to make us a campfire that Ol' Daniel Boone would have been proud of.

Being exhausted from the most difficult hike I had ever made, and Roy looking like a zombie, we hovered over our toasty firepit and stayed busy congratulating ourselves on our discovery. Even though there was only a light dusting of snow, so far, we knew that not all the Sasquatch were bedded down for the winter.

Reminding ourselves that our group had previously discussed at length, that our goal was to determine whether or not the Sasquatch hibernates were undoubtedly against all odds, as we had already seen that the animals were out and about. With the snow that had begun falling, we knew that we didn't have the time to wait much longer to find out whether or not they did or did not.

We had discussed this matter at great lengths, knowing that the best odds of learning the truth would be to await signs of their movement in the spring. The difficulty in that thinking however, was that it was not even conceivable that one could be anywhere near a hibernating creature at the exact moment it comes out of hibernation in the spring. The "where and when" could take a lifetime of study and still fail.

Gathering sticks, bark chunks and branches, we built up a strong fire in a way that when we awoke the next morning, we still had a good bed of coals. The night had been quiet and uneventful, and as we made a breakfast, we could finally see around us the extra-large hole the giant tree's roots had left when it toppled over. There was something different about this hole however; on the sides of this large excavation there seemed to be something wrong. Something just didn't fit. It was just a feeling like there was something different about the way the tree had uprooted. The roots on the upper stump appeared to have been cut, as the spidery roots so commonly found on uprooted trees were noticeably absent.

As we exited our shelter, we began walking among these monstrous behemoths, and it appeared that at one time there had to have been a tremendous windstorm that hit this mountain in order for it to topple so many trees. Something however was not making sense. I signaled Roy to join me as I walked further down the slope, stopping to more closely examine the fallen trees. They all seemed to have fallen in the same direction, but not all at the same time, and this slope was quite well protected from winds by the ridge nearby, so something wasn't adding up.

Then, we had an idea at the same time, and as we dropped into another hole, we found that it had a soft bottom! Beneath the dirt in the floor of the holes we now checked, we found that each contained an entire deep layer of pine boughs. Pulling up on one pile, it revealed itself to be several feet thick. We ran back to our shelter of the night before, and its floor was not at all like the other two.

Suddenly the reason became readily apparent. This tree still had a full complement of branches, and they were still green, as it had obviously recently fallen. A quick check of all the other downed trees showed they all had thick carpets of branches and pine needles packed deep on the floors.

We spent half the day searching this hillside, and then we went into another thick forest of several species of balsam and other evergreens that neither of us knew what they were, but in the thick forest of balsams, we found definite evidence that something had purposely dug up the entire one side of several individual trees, and it appeared that someone or something had been working diligently at severing and smashing the roots on only one side of the tree. Then we knew!

These Sasquatch had the superior intelligence to expend the effort to steadily weaken a tree to cause it to fall over, or in the large cases, to weaken the root structure so the next strong wind would cause it to topple. Then, in the late fall, the animals would gather boughs and leaves to pile into the holes where the roots had been, and await the coming of the first heavy snow while they rested under their warm blanket.

We decided to spend more time in this area rather than go any further up the mountain as had been our original plan after carefully analyzing the route we had intended to travel. Reason being, was we had only one goal when we began our climb, and it didn't make any sense to climb higher in search of some mystical cave or canyon where Sasquatch assembled to wait out the winter. That made no sense whatsoever to even think for a minute that an animal with the intelligence these creatures have already been proven to have, would gather in a group and risk perishing together in some bitter cold cave!

We began searching further, and in the dim light that managed to penetrate the thick blanket of pines, we slowly made our way downward, and we continued to find signs where certain trees had been dug out around their upper sides of their trunks, and there was evidence that the exposed roots had been smashed and cut through, and then they seemed to have then been covered with dead branches and pine needles to mask the progress of weakening the uphill support, so as to allow the constant mountain winds to eventually finish the job, and fell the tree in the direction the clever animals had predetermined.

This process of creating future shelters seemed at first to be a painstakingly slow process, but as we discussed throughout our search; the obviously slow birth rate suspected among this species would not make it necessary to rush the process, and we found evidence in several instances that were obviously more recent diggings, due to the fact that there were massive amounts of needles still clinging to the branches, and that drew us to more closely inspect the massive root balls. We found that in many cases where needles remained thick on branches of felled trees, that the enormous root systems showed signs of fresh cuts which we have deduced to be evidence confirming our theory that, although no longer standing, somehow these root systems may have been covered by the Sasquatch to keep them alive and still nourishing the host tree, even as it lay dormant and dying.

At first, this made no sense, but then, we found more evidence that something seemed to have chewed on many of these attached roots. Our first reaction had been that squirrels were actively eating these roots, but the few squirrels we had seen at this altitude had easier pickings in the safety of the tree branches, and it is common knowledge that squirrels prefer deciduous trees, so it was not even conceivable that the squirrels would risk themselves to seek out the roots of dying pine trees.

Having eliminated that thought, we began to more closely examine several more of these root balls, and after hours more climbing in and out of several more holes and sifting through the floors of these holes, we have reached what we believe to be absolute proof that the Sasquatch does indeed hibernate!

We further state our belief, that this elusive species hibernates together as a family unit. Judging from our many excavations, there is adequate evidence that these creatures, in most cases, wait until the first heavy snowfall covers the entire forest in a deep blanket of permanent covering; the young ones, due to the evidence of smaller teeth marks, will often nibble on the living roots in their chamber prior to completely sleeping for the winter. This may be a way of slowly easing into hibernation until the heaver snows seal their hideaway!

Further evidence helped prove our theory when the huge trees had fallen where the terrain had caused the root ball to have broken all of the roots completely. These holes had no evidence of any occupancy whatsoever. We concluded that the nesting chambers of the Bigfoot are carefully chosen by them in advance, and part of their consideration may be that they prefer live root systems.

We also found what seemed like piles of boughs, that in each case, had been torn off live trees of other species; that showed evidence that the bark had been chewed off, as these branches seemed to have been collected, as humans would, to bring nighttime snacks into the bedroom. A strange analogy, but the Sasquatch seem to have many habits similar to humans.

We reasoned also that these food sources would perhaps have been to assist the animals' transition into hibernation. My partner's remarks of "Sasquatch snacks" still makes a lot of sense. At least it seemed to in sub-zero temperatures.

We made camp a ways back in a patch of balsams that were out of sight of this obvious Sasquatch territory and had a rather fitful sleep which we both attributed to being in the home of these giant creatures brought on sleep inducing stress, as we half expected to be attacked at any moment!

We awoke to a blanket of white. An unexpected early snowfall, that from the accumulation already covering our boot soles, we took the hint and packed up to return to our base camp. This was definitely the beginning of winter.

Roy agreed with my assessment, as he had grown up in this country, and he said the last weather report he had heard told of a probability for an early snowfall, which this late in the season, it would likely stay, so it made sense for us not to stay.

The snow was falling heavier now, and both of us were entirely focused on placing our every step when suddenly Roy's arm shot out to block my next step, and as I raised my eyes to the trail ahead, a dark shape ducked immediately into the darkness of the forest. All Roy whispered was "Bigfoot," and we continued to where the tracks of the animal were rapidly blending into the white blanket of snow.

We knew that trying to pursue the creature would be fruitless, so we continued downward while an occasional backward glance briefly caught a glimpse of the dark shadow as the Sasquatch again stepped out to resume its trek up the trail.

Having been alerted, we now paid more heed to the trail further down, and on several more occasions, we caught quick glimpses of dark shapes against the now much whiter background.

Eventually, we made it out once more into the open where we could again see blue sky. We gave each other a "high five," because we had just confirmed what we had long suspicioned. That the Sasquatch prepared their winter quarters and then remained somewhat active at lower elevations until they sensed the coming of the first major snowfall of the season. And once it began, they moved into their preselected winter quarters at the higher elevations where they were assured that the winter would set in solidly for the season. They seemed to wait until the very last minute to assure that there was no chance of being discovered in their winter chambers.

We finally made it to the low enough altitude where the snow had not yet fallen, and there were Jerry and Bill, and as if they had known we were coming, they were all packed and ready to go.

We wasted no time in heading out, and as we started at a quick pace downward, a light sprinkle of snow began to fall, as if to discourage us from changing our minds. After all, we were the only things on this mountain that didn't belong!

# GRANDFATHER'S TWO SECRETS

## By A.J.

Growing up in Oregon, I never gave much thought to the stories my classmates brought to school, and our teachers had a firm rule against discussing any stories related to Sasquatch and Bigfoot. We had been indoctrinated from an early age that these creatures were never to be discussed, as it would cause people from the rest of America to move to Oregon, and our parents would no longer be able to live here due to overcrowding. I wonder now if all the teachers in our state also created this fear?

Beginning at so young an age, we all just naturally kept our family secrets to ourselves, at least as far as teachers were concerned. I guess it's not any different than hiding family embarrassments from others, so I never thought a whole lot about it. That is; until it happened to me! My mother was a teacher at our local school, so I had to be especially careful about discussions around the dinner table, lest I annoy my very opinionated mother.

We had many Sasquatch believers in our extended family, so I had a lot of secrets to keep, and even though I was unfamiliar with them, I was taught to accept them as I would any living creature that I knew lived around the area; even though there were many species I had never seen, as it was with Sasquatch so far at that time.

Our community was no different from others in this wildly beautiful country, and we were very protective of our lifestyle, and our secret animal was protected by a population who had no desire to attract visitors searching our mountains. Our adult population seemed to be totally against increasing our population, and they always made reference to not being like California.

This long lead-in will perhaps explain why my grandfather had been able to keep his secret from all of our extended family, and how I came to be the only one besides maybe my grandmother to learn of it!

I had just graduated from high school, and I was planning to enjoy one final summer vacation before going into the military. Grandfather came by the house to invite me to spend a week with him at his and Grandmother's cabin near the Illinois River; near where it joins the famous Rogue River to make their way to the Pacific Ocean.

I felt very honored that he had invited me, because none of my cousins had ever been invited to even see the property, and here was my chance to spend an entire week. Grandmother had been feeling poorly for a while, so she declined to come along to what she called the "woods," so with my bag packed with hiking clothes I couldn't wait. Even the discomfort of Grandfather's old Jeep Wrangler on the seemingly neglected county road was pleasureful to me. The county rarely maintained this dead-end stretch of the loneliest section of the wild corner of where almost no-one lived. Grandfather's only neighbor was a crusty old bachelor who had a whole line of "keep out" signs all along his property, and since Grandfather's land was the last place on the road, no one probably realized there was even a house there, as he didn't even have mail delivery due to the inconvenience of having to check both locations, here and in town.

So, here we were after a lot of bouncing in the Jeep that Grandfather must have forgotten had any brakes, as he never thought to slow down for bumps in the poorly maintained road. I had the duty of unlocking the huge gate, and after Grandfather passed through, I closed and locked it behind us. The cabin sat in the back of the forest of pine trees that Grandfather had planted when he first bought it and had the house built. Once parked by the back door, the Jeep was totally hidden from the road, and even the smoke from the fireplace took a route behind the hill to the Illinois River only a quarter mile away. I had stayed here a few times in the past, so I had been more than a little excited about this trip!

As we sat on the picnic table after wiping off a month's

supply of pine needles and relaxing with cokes; Grandfather grew serious, and he consciously lowered his voice, as he leaned forward and looking directly at the spot between my eyes, he asked, "What do you know about Sasquatch?"

I was shocked by the seriousness and the manner in which he asked, and I stammered to reply that I knew what they were, when he continued without waiting for my reply. Saying that he had allowed a family of them to live on his property, and had for many years!

Then, he began a more casual tone as he went into great detail about how they had first made contact, and his long process of leaving various foods for them, and pretty much of a history dating back to when he and Grandmother first had the cabin built, and how it took several years before my Grandmother dared go with him to what he called their "Hideout!" He explained that he had still never told Grandmother about these Sasquatch, because she would have refused to ever return.

I sat enthralled with the stories of his experiences, and the thought entered my mind as to why he had never before brought up the subject, even those times when I had stayed here for a couple of days at a time. Without me even having to ask, Grandfather explained that his "friends" were too precious to take any chances with their security, so he waited until he felt I had matured to disclose his precious secret.

I had a feeling of great pride that in the eyes of such a wise and respected retired county judge now considered me with the respect of his trust. He told me that he was going to teach me two secrets that only he knew, and I would be expected to keep everything confidential and reveal the information to no one else.

As he spoke, he reached into the canvas bag he had nonchalantly placed beside him when we first sat down, and pulled out a quart sized Mason jar and set it before me on the table. It was full of gold! I picked it up, and I was amazed at how heavy it was. I could barely heft it chest high to stare at the contents.

Grandfather then told me that no one besides the two of us now knew the secret that he had successfully kept from everyone, and after he had discovered the gold source accidently while fishing, he had purchased the land and built the cabin, although Grandmother had never gone near the river because of her hatred of mosquitoes, she had enjoyed the times spent here.

Grandfather explained that there was no way to file a gold claim, as the government had banned any more mining claims years before. Also, in order to sell his gold with no questions asked, his friend and fishing buddy, who also panned gold nearby, set up contact with a source in California's "black market," and this was their way of selling the gold without any records. Grandfather said that this source also paid a lot more for larger nuggets that could be made into jewelry, which was all the more reason to deal out of the area, so no jealous rival would turn him into the authorities.

At first, I thought that their main reason may have been to avoid paying tax, because finding gold is not illegal, and when I questioned him on that, Grandfather was quick to point out that it had been necessary to keep every association with gold discovery totally hidden, as there were still cases on the books of missing persons who had discovered gold, and after selling it through regular means and paying the state and federal taxes, they had suddenly disappeared! He said people who would never have even considered being crooked will do strange things for a gold claim.

Then I could understand, as I had always heard from friends whose fathers worked in law enforcement that Oregon has a high number of "missing persons" on the record books; some dating way back to the 1800's where men just "vanished!" That happened quite often to newcomers.

I had to smile when I thought back to those "dinner-table discussions" my parents had over the years, where they expressed concerns about my grandparents maybe being heavily in debt, and how they may have to step in to help financially if either of them became sick. Thinking back to those discussions, I had to grin, and I had done so subconsciously, as Grandfather caught me; so I had to explain. I think he laughed for the rest of the day, because every once in a while, he snickered, just thinking about it! Then, he told me in confidence that my folks would really be shocked if they knew the huge sum of money they stood to inherit!

I remembered how I had heard them worrying when he bought the new Cadillac, and then the Jeep. I bet they would really be shocked at the brand new 4-wheel drive, three quarter ton pickup that he kept in the garage that still had the window sticker on it. I chuckled aloud at the secrets only Grandfather and I knew.

Then, Grandfather grew really serious as he leaned forward and began speaking in a lower tone, as if there was a chance of being overheard, and at first, I thought that he was doing it for show, however he was very sincere when he reminded me of the time when I had been in the garage on one of my stays with he and Grandmother; he had sent me to the garage for a can of assorted nails, and there were two identical cans, so I opened them both, and the one had a pint sized glass jar full of gold. When I brought out the nails, I asked Grandfather if it was really gold, and he said it was and then swore me to secrecy. As he again spoke, he confessed that his finding that gold so long ago was no accident; and in fact, that had been a test to see if I could keep a secret, and he apologized for doing that, but he said that it was extremely important that I passed, because now, he was going to show me the most important secret of all! A secret that I had to swear to keep, as long as he was alive, and only after he was gone, could I tell anyone about what he was about to share with me.

Grandfather then began a short critique of the state, and how they put giant steel gates across every public access road and how they treat the public lands as if it was their personal property by randomly closing these beautiful forests to all comers. He said they claim it's to prevent forest fires, but he felt it was just their way of cutting their workload, so they could spend more time sitting around and drawing their paychecks by filing phony reports. So, with mountains full of gold that recreational miners would enjoy finding and earning a few dollars from, they selfishly let it lie.

I listened without speaking, and with the occasional nod, Grandfather unloaded his frustrations, and it sounded familiar, because my friend's fathers had often spoken about similar disappointments, as living in "gold country" without being able to even pan a small amount is certainly a disappointment.

I sat enthralled by stories of Grandfather's mining friends who held original "grandfathered gold claims), who didn't even dare to go into town for supplies, because if they left their claims unguarded, the state people would sneak in and burn their cabins and dynamite their claims; and when he finally leaned back and realized that perhaps he needed to mellow out, I had a clear understanding of why he had kept his secret so well. I had heard a similar story from my high school coach whose father had owned a mine.

Grandfather got back to why he had felt it so important that I understood his reasons for secrecy, and then he began telling me about the secret source of his gold, and why he had felt it was time that he included someone he could trust to carry on profiting from his find, after he was gone. He must have noticed my furled brow, because he quickly assured me that he was in good health, but he felt better having a "partner."

I swelled with pride as he placed the jar of gold back in its hiding place, handed me a backpack, shouldered an even larger one, and making sure the cabin and garage were locked, he strapped on a shell belt and holster containing his magnum revolver, and we started walking into the thick forest behind the garage.

Exiting through a small gate, he closed it behind us and within minutes, all signs of civilization were gone. Not even airplanes passed over this area, unless from a small coastal town, so in only a few minutes, we were in a different world!

As we walked at a steady pace on the well-traveled animal trail, Grandfather reminisced about when he and his friend had first discovered this gold, and he again told me how sad it was when his longtime pal had suffered that fatal heart attack, and he had no living relatives, so Grandfather had handled all funeral arrangements. I vaguely remembered hearing about it from my folks conversations.

As we continued meandering on this trail, the sound of the Illinois River was becoming louder, and it was soon impossible to carry on a conversation without raising our voices which we did not wish to attempt, lest we should be overheard. Walking quietly in the forest is a most enjoyable experience.

The sounds of the river were greatly diminished now as Grandfather explained that it was now on a direct course to where it would soon flow into the famous Rogue River that was only a few miles from here.

This was such a treacherous section of the Illinois River that Grandfather said you could be standing on the shore, and very seldom would you ever even be noticed by a single rafter, as at this point, they would be totally concentrating on staying alive. All of a sudden; as if to prove his point, we heard a mingling of shouts and screams, and around the bend came a huge rubber raft that swayed violently through the churning and frothing white water, and it was a wonder that the ropes they had around them could keep them seated as the four people paddled in desperation when the huge raft raised up almost perpendicular to the ground as they finally passed through the rough rapids, and then the river ran straight for another fifty yards and then curved sharply to the left, and the shouting commenced once more as they disappeared around the bend. Grandfather pointed out the fact that not one of the four had even glanced our way; and at that point, he stopped abruptly and turned toward the cliff that loomed high above our left side, and without a word, he grabbed hold of an old rotting snag that I thought was rooted to the sand beneath it, but it came away easily to reveal a very narrow crack in the wall of the cliff. Without a word, Grandfather motioned for me to enter, and then, when we were inside, he carefully rocked the snag back into its previous spot and tossed a handful of dry sand at the base so it once again looked as if it was rooted there. Within a few feet, the narrow slot widened into a sort of shoulder-level passageway that the smooth sides indicated an ancient lava flow that Grandfather said had passed through this area and left a myriad of these rocky rivulets that all seemed to feed into the Illinois and the Rogue rivers.

In the very center of this short-walled slot ran a stream that was crystal clear, and the bottom of which was gravel and smaller rock that the centuries had worn smooth; and I could see many pieces of what looked like obsidian and crystals, and then at a wider spot around another slight bend, Grandfather stopped suddenly and removed his pack, indicating with a nod for me to follow suit. Placing my pack beside his, I watched as he withdrew a well concealed bag, and from the waterproof rubber container, he withdrew two small folding army shovels and two black plastic pans that I instantly recognized were for panning gold because of the built-in ridges.

In only a couple of minutes, I had learned the art of proper panning for gold. I knelt there staring at several tiny specks of gold amidst the fine black sand that covered the bottom of my pan.

Then, Grandfather seeming pleased that I had mastered the art so quickly; opened up his pack and brought out our lunch. There we sat, on opposite sides of the small stream, enjoying the sun that was chasing away the chill of the morning, and then Grandfather told me the story of how he and his best friend had accidentally stumbled onto this hidden slot when they were fishing from the bank when a storm suddenly rolled in. He said it rained so hard that they had wedged themselves up close to the bank when the old-dead tree broke off at the bottom to reveal the narrow slot canyon behind it, and they slipped around it, as it still was connected by the roots. As they sheltered in the protection of the walls where we now sat; his partner had noticed a gold glint when the sun finally took control of the weather and that caused them to become instant goldminers. Grandfather made me swear an oath to never reveal to anyone what we shared while he was alive; which I proudly swore to.

Next, something happened that almost scared me so badly that I felt silly like a girl afterwards. There came a sort of a shriek, like the monkeys in Tarzan movies made, and it was loud enough that I suddenly lurched back and hit my head on the rock wall when Grandfather held up his hand and put his finger to his lips to caution me, and he nodded as if to say it was "all right."

Then as he withdrew a large plastic wrapped package from his pack, my curiosity was answered as to why he shouldered such an oversized pack. He placed the large, and apparently heavy package on a place on the ridge above him, and then he sat back down, and once again gave me the sign to remain silent.

Then, I felt like the first time I saw the movie "King Kong" as this giant fur covered creature suddenly loomed directly above Grandfather's head, and Grandfather turned slightly to acknowledge the giant Sasquatch without getting to his feet, and the huge creature then looked at me, and then it seemed to furl its brow as it looked back at Grandfather. Grandfather returned its curious stare with a nod and he pointed his open hand at me, and then back to his chest once more, and the Sasquatch then nodded his head at Grandfather, and then, looking at me once again he repeated that nod, to which I took the hint and also nodded in return. Somehow this seemed to me as an introduction, and a sort of acceptance by the big animal that, as Grandfather later told me, he was depending on me to continue this strange friendship after he was gone! I readily agreed that I would gladly do so and then he told me that he would give me a written list of what goodies I should bring, and what times of the year, and then he shocked me into open-mouthed silence by his next statement. He said that he had invited me as a test to confirm a major decision he had made, and then he really gave me a jolt. Grandfather said that in the next few days he was planning to file and record his will, and in it, I was listed to be the sole recipient of his cabin and all possessions on the property! He said he had discussed this decision with Grandmother, since she would never come here without him, and she was in total agreement.

I went through the mental shock and the emotions that I guessed were natural in such circumstances, and he explained that this was not as big a gift as it may seem, because he was "dead serious" that above all else, his Sasquatch friends must be taken care of!

So now, I guess my future has been pretty much decided, as from Grandfather's notes and the sources he will soon be introducing me to for selling my gold, Grandfather and I will be working together around the cabin, and at times working our gold claim, but I will continue living my life, and he will hopefully live a long time, but what an exciting future I will have. Wait until my parents find out I have planned my future without their help! The only thing I'll need is a regular job as well.

The one other thing that we agreed on, is that I will be present on all future trips to the Sasquatch family, which are most frequent in the summer months, and as yet, Grandfather is still not certain if they hibernate, but he seldom sees them in the mid-winter months, but he has trouble at that time of year due to the sporadic snows, so he said that so far, he had not heard any objection from the Sasquatch. Then he laughed loudly, and it was quite a funny thought at that.

My only problem when telling you this for publication in your next book, is that I am bursting inside with my secret that I cannot disclose to anyone. I can only allow for you to use this under some fictitious name when I would like to tell the whole world, but the safety factor that holds me in check is that I will be well compensated for my silence.

As we discussed; I plan to send you a future story as my relationship with the Sasquatch progresses, and I'll use the identity code that I sign-off with (undisclosed).

# MY UNCLE'S SASQUATCH

By Tim

*Publisher's note: This submission resulted from an encounter with Sasquatch by the brother of an old friend of ours in Oregon, and came about from their having read our book, "Hiking Sasquatch Country."*

*Our friend's brother had been visiting his uncle in the town of Rogue River, Oregon only a few miles from the infamous "Rogue River" that is in the top five or so of the world's wildest rivers.*

*We'll call him "Tim" for privacy concerns; his story was really interesting to us, as another friend of ours had encountered a Sasquatch in roughly the same area only two years before.*

*Tim had purchased our book not knowing that his brother Tony was our friend, and when Tony saw our names, he still had my cellphone number and gave us a call; it was great to hear from him again as we hadn't seen him since we moved to the desert.*

*So then I phoned Tim and he gave us the story, and with few geographical changes, this is Tim's personal story.*

I went to visit my Uncle Barry in the town of Rogue River, Oregon; which is only a short way from the California border. Uncle Barry had recently lost his wife in a boating accident at their cabin on the Rogue River, and he had called my mother to see if I would be willing to take a trip over from our home in Klamath Falls to go with him to the cabin, as he was afraid to drive there by himself as he was still morning the loss of Aunt June. So, since I was off my teaching job for another month, I agreed. Besides, I was always fascinated by the beauty of Western Oregon's forests, and figured maybe I could get in a few hikes. So before I headed west, I bought a book titled, "Hiking Sasquatch Country;" which seemed quite appropriate. Mom agreed to check on my apartment while I was gone, and up Highway 140 I went; a grueling trip to say the least.

When I arrived, I was really happy to see how well Uncle Barry was taking the loss of Aunt June, and he seemed glad to have me there, as he had never before stayed there alone.

The third day I was there, we climbed in Uncle Barry's aged Willy's Jeep that he kept in meticulous condition, although I found it to be the most uncomfortable vehicle I had ever ridden in, and I was ever so happy when we finally arrived after being bounced around so much on what I guess Barry had stated was a road, but the "road" had ended at a locked gate to his property. We went through, and I don't know how he found the trail through the overgrown grasses, but finally we pulled up beside a surprisingly nice cabin. It had been built of split logs and it had a shake roof which Barry said would last a lifetime. To me, it looked like it already had!

I could see that my uncle kept dabbing at his eyes with his handkerchief, and I found myself doing the same as we stepped inside the musty cabin. Soon, we had the windows open, and the pleasant smell of pines wafted through the cabin.

After we unpacked, I was anxious to see his short wooden dock, as he had told me that Aunt June had slipped off the dock when he was headed back with some snacks, as they liked to sit and wave at the steady flow of rafters that came down river only minutes apart.

The flow of rafts went continuously throughout daylight hours, and there was seldom time enough for all but a quick wave of the hand as they fought the raging current. Most of them never looked up long enough to know we were even there.

Barry grew tearful as he told how he had not returned from the cabin in time, as he heard June scream, and she was already gone before he made it down to the dock.

To take his mind off of the loss of Aunt June, I quickly changed the subject. My mom had already told me that the authorities found June's body ten miles downstream. I asked Barry to show me around the property, and he seemed glad to walk among the trees as we strolled around the sizeable lot.

Later, over the next couple of days, Barry grew more relaxed, and we began a regimen of walks along the rugged riverside, on a well-used river trail, and I noticed how when we were up top near the cabin, Barry always cut our walks well before where I knew his property line was. It went on for at least another several hundred yards where there was no longer a road, but instead, the entire area all along the river was thick with large pines, balsams and firs; and from what I could tell, it was beautiful! I could see in the distance where his fence ended, but still, we didn't go near.

I really wanted to go further on, but every time I wanted to continue, Uncle Barry found some excuse why we had to return to the cabin.

One day, on a regular walk, we went a bit further than normal, and I caught a glimpse of a familiar object; a large gunny sack that I recognized as one of the items we had brought with us. Then, with what seemed almost like a sign of relief, Uncle Barry confessed.

He motioned me toward a couple of old, half-rotted logs of huge diameter, and he sat down, gesturing for me to take a seat on the large log across from him. Uncle Barry leaned forward and spoke low enough that I had to lean in to hear him even though we were only a few feet apart. Then he told me he had a confession to make.

He began by telling me that my Aunt June was the only person besides himself to even know what he was about to tell me now, and then he pointed to the gunny sack that he knew I had recognized. He said that every morning since we had arrived, he had gotten up early and left an offering of food for his "friends," and then he brought the empty bag back before I was up. This morning, he had forgotten to retrieve it.

He began to shake slightly as he made me swear that I would never tell another soul what he was about to reveal; which I readily agreed to, and then he told me that a couple of generations of Sasquatch lived in the area beyond where he always left the "goodies." My jaw felt like it was unhinged as I leaned further forward with my mouth open.

Uncle Barry explained that shortly after he and June had bought this land and cabin for a vacation retreat, June had placed a couple of pies on the, now leaning, picnic table to cool, and when she went out to retrieve them, they were gone. She got pretty scared that it might have been a bear, so Uncle Barry had June carry his shotgun, and he held his 30-30 Winchester rifle as they easily followed the bent grass up the slight grade along the river. The noise of the river was enough to mute their footsteps and they found the ground to be covered only lightly by sparse grasses, and they were careful to avoid stepping on the dead pine branches that littered the ground as they walked in a crouch.

Aunt June suddenly dropped to her knees and told Barry there was a bear up ahead. Barry said he looked where she was pointing, and it looked like the bear was standing erect, and there was another one sitting upright by the next tree.

That was when they realized that the creatures were the Sasquatch the previous owners had told them about!

Barry said that even though they had heard about the Bigfoot animals when they first arrived in the area, being native Iowans, they dismissed the stories as something made up to scare tourists away. Oregon had long held a reputation for being quite hostile to anyone wishing to locate here.

Then, one of the Sasquatch seemed to pass its pie tin to the other one, and that's when they realized that the creatures had been eating with their hands, and wild animals don't casually lean against trees with their legs stretched out! Barry said that he and June must have lost their "cool" and made a gasp or some noise, as the creatures stood erect and ran into the thick pines that he now motioned towards.

Anyway, I was enthralled by the continuation of their relationship that they developed with these animals; although they always kept their distances, over time, they left treats and different fruits and vegetables for the Sasquatch at the same place as I now was staring at.

Barry pointed to a large, but gnarly and weathered apple tree that Aunt June had him plant just for these "neighbors," and Barry said they always picked it clean of every new apple. I could see that this new, thick crop was beginning to ripen.

After June passed away, Barry said he stopped coming out here, but it was just before he called to invite me up for a visit when he remembered his promise to June to look after her "furry neighbors." He said he hadn't dared to make the first trip by himself.

Well, I was thoroughly exited, and like most guys, I wanted to attempt a close contact, and I had all the desire to see if I could get some photos as I had my camera in my bag, but Uncle Barry shot me down on that idea, as he had promised June to never allow any news of these friends to get out, and I had to respect that, although reluctantly.

So, we stayed there another week during which time we caught and ate fish, sat for hours watching the crashing caldrons of water speeding toward the Pacific, and did a few repairs on the cabin. All-in-all, we both enjoyed being alone with nature and reminiscing about the past.

Barry made me promise to return the following summer, and as we were loading up the Jeep, I saw from the corner of my eye, a quick movement, and I turned to see the two Sasquatch, and alongside them were two small ones that had to be their offspring; I judged the small ones to be about four feet high. And then for a final thrill, I waved farewell, and all four of them mimicked my action. Then they disappeared into the forest once more, and I turned to see Barry with his extended arm still in the air.

I'm going back!

# WONDERING IF ZANE GREY SAW SASQUATCH

By Tad

*Publisher's note: When Wendy and I were on the board of directors for the Josephine County Historical Society in Grants Pass, Oregon, Wendy was able to arrange for our society to sell copies of many books in order for us to raise necessary funds for our many charitable events.*

*The most famous of these publications was a book titled, "The Rogue: A River to Run." It was written by Florence Armon, and it is the fascinating life story about Glen Wooldridge who was the first man to have run the famous Rogue River all the 120 miles from Grants Pass to the Pacific Ocean! That was long before the massive dynamiting of the man killing boulders that made the Rogue River one of the most dangerous rivers in the world!*

*Glen Wooldridge became world famous for his exploits, and he personally guided famous celebrities such as Zane Grey, Clark Gable, President Herbert Hoover and hundreds of their peers down the mighty Rogue. He made himself and the Rogue River famous.*

*Renowned author Zane Grey had a cabin built on the north bank of the wild river, complete with his own private airstrip, to which he himself piloted his single engine plane to spend time fishing and relaxing. The book entitled, "Rogue River Feud" was the result of one long stay where the famous author could really and totally relax while he wrote the novel.*

*This brings us to the visitor who came to an event at the historical society while we were on the board. (I wonder if when I was president if the name changed to president of the bored?)*

*Anyway, our visitor, whom we will call "Tad," short for Theodore, had a really interesting story that involved his own adventure on the "Wild Rogue" when he and a friend had attempted to ride the terribly dangerous river, with the intention to meet the famous author, and also run the famous river from Grants Pass to the Pacific Ocean. This adventure happened many years back when Glen Wooldridge had yet to retire.*

*He explained that he and his friend were hoping beyond any reasonable expectation that they might at least get their names in the paper, and maybe even get a better job than working the night shift at the famous Almeda gold mine.*

*Tad handed us a story of his and his friend Larry's adventure that Tad's sister, Helena, had typed for him, and so we were able to make our own notes on what he agreed was a rambling bunch of individual events of their various frustrations.*

*What follows is a condensed version of their wild adventure, as told by Tad.*

Our goal was to find and visit with the famous western novelist, Zane Grey, at his cabin on the mighty Rogue River. A policeman friend in Grants Pass had told us a ranger had seen Mr. Grey's plane land at his cabin, and since we had just begun a week-long vacation from our job at the Almeda, we thought maybe we could meet the author, and maybe, somehow become famous ourselves. Dumb thought, but we were young enough yet to believe in miracles. After all, nobody had shot us yet, so we figured we were lucky!

We real quick filled a couple of cloth sacks with sandwiches, soda pop and potato chips, along with our two sleeping bags and a big tarp we borrowed from Larry's father. Larry also sneaked his dad's .22 revolver into his pack and I had brought my own .25 caliber pistol my uncle had loaned me for the summer, along with an extra box of cartridges.

We knew that the guns wouldn't do much damage to a bear, but we hoped if one came along, we would scare it away. The authorities didn't worry much back then, as there wasn't nearly as much traffic on the river as there is now. Besides that, even after the dynamiting of the really dangerous rocks, the river remained one of the most treacherous rivers in the world.

After a couple of hours, we were getting exhausted. It was a whole lot harder to control the raft than we had thought, even though Larry had been rafting a few times before, he had forgot how to keep the raft going straight, so we kept having to fight to keep it so we could watch for rocks and rapids as we swayed around.

The day was sunny, but the constant spray of water from our paddles swinging back and forth to stop us spinning, made us shiver even with our jackets on.

We finally agreed to make an early camp, and since we were

practically exhausted, we pulled over on the south side of the river where a small sort of a cove had some soft looking sand along the shore. Being careful with the raft, we emptied it and then pulled it up on the grassy bank and tied the rope around a tree to keep it from being blown back in the river.

Back in those days, we got by with making a firepit down near the water and we lined it with rocks. We had several hours 'til sundown, so we spent the time tying up our lean-to and weighting the other end down with rocks, and with our sleeping bags laid out under it, we had a very pleasant campsite.

We had been tempted to bring beer, but we decided it was too important a trip to have liquor on our breaths if we met Zane Grey. We talked at length about how we would introduce ourselves and that we could offer to help out doing chores around his cabin, and maybe cutting firewood for him, and we pictured maybe meeting somebody like Clark Gable, and then as young men will do, we pictured us maybe being in a movie, and when it finally came to sundown, we must have fallen asleep over exhaustion from all of those movie rolls we had been offered.

Sometime in the night, I woke up shivering, as the cold wind seemed to be blowing harder than it had been, so I added a few chunks of tree limbs to the embers that still glowed in the bottom of our firepit, and soon, I had a nice warm fire once more, and Larry stirred enough to roll over and go back to sleep.

I lit up a cigarette, and I sat their watching the moon through the lofty pines standing guard overhead, when suddenly as they say, "All hell broke loose!" The firepit seemed to explode; ashes were flying in all directions and a large shadowy figure went crashing through our camp, knocking our lean-to into the trees behind me, with the support sticks flying, and small fires were starting up everywhere under the monstrously tall pines. I saw Larry batting at his hair and clothes, as I was, while at the same time, stomping about in our bare feet to avoid the hot ashes that were everywhere!

Suddenly, the very real fear of being attacked by a bear gave rise to us both retrieving our handguns, and while I fumbled with my holster snap, Larry's revolver began spitting fire with loud reports and muzzle flashes that added to the confusion, while I stood ready at last, holding my minute pistol. From the size of the monster that wrecked our camp, I remember hoping that Larry didn't hit it. It turned out that Larry also had the same fear after seeing the size of the animal, so he had purposely shot into the dirt behind camp.

Neither of us had been in the slightest bit prepared for what had happened, because we relaxed in the security of an animal's fear of fire. What we hadn't reckoned with, was the faint possibility that these Sasquatch creatures were actually real, nor the remote chance that we would ever see one!

Now, we concluded beyond any doubt that a Sasquatch had indeed been what had scared years off of our lives! We built up the fire even more, and gathered more rocks to build up its perimeter, but neither of us dared to fall back asleep; not that we could anyway.

As the sun finally brought light to our camp, we finished straightening up, and we rebuilt our fire to cut the morning chill, and that was when we noticed one of our backpacks was missing. Searching all around the area, we had to conclude that our visitor grabbed it as it went crashing through.

That pack held most of our food and our camera, as well as our two boxes of extra ammunition for our feeble handguns. Not that we figured they would be anywhere near any protection against our giant visitor, but also for security against our fellow man, as more and more transients were settling into our area and camping out in our forests.

Armed now with the three remaining cartridges in Larry's revolver and the six in my pistol, we decided it might be time to head to the nearest take-out point downriver and hitch a ride back to Grants Pass on one of the shuttles. We were really tired now from the previous day, the interruption of our sleep, and the exhaustion from being traumatized by the Sasquatch.

Suddenly, as we floated in the calmer waters, there on the bank about a hundred or so feet away was the Sasquatch that wrecked our camp! We knew it was the one, because in its massive paw was our backpack!

The only comical part of our whole trip was when Larry yelled out to it and hollered for it to "at least take our picture, since it had the camera!" The animal only snorted in reply and ducked into the brush.

Focusing back on the river once more, Larry's head suddenly whipped to look at the north bank of the river, to which I also looked, and there was what had to be Zane Grey's cabin, and a few yards away was a single engine Piper Cub airplane that could only mean that our entire trip had been for naught!

There was no chance we could cross the fierce rapids in enough time to reach that far shore, as by the time we could have made it, we would have to walk back several long miles under the steep cliffs that bordered the river at this point, and there was not even a visible shore anywhere near. Also, the curve in the river was forcing us to the left.

Our mutual disappointment was obvious as we just held our paddles on our laps and floated in the fast-moving current. Now all we had to do is fight hard to find some motivation to go back to work at the Almeda gold mine!

# HOME FOR SALE; SASQUATCH INCLUDED

By Peg B.

Sometimes being honest with people just makes no sense. I say that because we had listed our home on the Oregon coast for sale three months earlier, and we had not received even one offer. We are located just south of Brookings, and although Highway 101 lay between us and the ocean, we owned 37 acres of mostly pine trees except for our small garden and a miniature orchard with a few fruit trees.

We had lived on the place for over 40 years, and the few houses nearby had changed hands a few times, but usually by retirees, and they had sold rather quickly. So when we decided to move into a senior care center due to mobility problems, we thought selling our property would be an easy matter, so we called a friend of our son's who works for a local real estate agency; we'll call him Tom.

Well, Tom was already familiar with our home as he had sold homes all around us over the years, and his own father had been friends with our builder, so it was easy. Maybe I should say, "too easy," as after eight long months we still had not had a single offer.

People would come along with Tom or another realtor, and they all, for the most part, seemed to love the property, but that would be the end of it. There wasn't one offer!

Knowing that we were reaching our limit of patience; Tom came over one day to have a sit-down with us, because we had already lowered our asking price on two different occasions, but to no avail. Tom had never brought it up before, but as we went over the entire procedure, all the way to the point where Tom would politely excuse himself to give the buyers time to visit with us privately. He was shaking his head, trying to find something that kept killing the sales, and although he said that he inquired of each buyer as to why they didn't want the house, they never gave any good reason, and he had sold each one of them a different home.

Tom was preparing to leave when he turned back around and asked if maybe something in our private sit-down with the buyers was causing them to leave without so much as an offer, so we agreed to role-play with him. We went over the typical conversation, and he was still shaking his head when I got to the part about the Sasquatch, and his eyes got wide as he asked us exactly what we were saying to people. I just told him that we would tell the people that if they bought our home, we hoped they would continue to care for the family of Sasquatch that lived way back in the forest. We would tell them the food items that we occasional brought from the store, and that the fruit trees out back had been planted after we first moved in and how the Sasquatch family enjoyed them. Then we would assure the people that the animals were friendly, and they only came out in the nicer weather when there was not as much rain. Then, they would all seem to leave happy.

Tom suddenly startled us when he threw back his head and

raised his arms up high above him and said, "That's it!" Tom seemed almost beside himself as he kept shaking his head, and I know he was blaming us for the fact the house hadn't sold even though he didn't say so. We had a long discussion about future customers, and we finally, but reluctantly, agreed that we would not discuss the Sasquatch. Although we felt it was our personal obligation to protect the poor creatures that had been like our pets all of these years, we needed desperately to sell!

About a week later, we finally had a couple show up with Tom, and after he gave them the tour and answered all of their questions, he stepped out to allow us a private visit as normal, only this time it was different. After we told the folks how much we had enjoyed living here, they gave us their background. They had lived their entire lives in the Los Angeles suburbs, and had studied for the last three years to select a place to retire, and they decided the Oregon coast would be the place for them.

Then, the lady made a statement I will never forget. She said, "Our dream home, although it will never come true, would be to live near where your famous Bigfoot live so we could actually see one!" My husband threw up his arms and he laughed so hard he began choking, and as I got up to go to his aid, he waved me off, and there he was laughing and slapping his legs while the people just stared. Then, when he regained his composure, he apologized profusely and pointed to the door, saying for me to call Tom in; which I did.

The buyers were sitting there looking confused when Tom came in and took a chair facing all of us, and I said, "Now Tom, we want you to tell these nice people about the secret that you made us agree to no longer mention to people about our neighbors." The look on Tom's face was as funny as it was seriously doubting what he had heard me say! He timidly asked if I meant "Sasquatch," to which we all laughed. After that, we went in to detail of our encounters with them; as many as we could remember.

Anyway, the sale happened quickly, and in thinking back, perhaps I should have early on found a better way to test whether or not something like a Sasquatch living on the property might be alarming.

It has been six months since we sold, and yesterday, we met our buyers in the store, and when they saw us, they rushed over to tell us about their first meeting with our Sasquatch; and incidentally, they were buying a large number of pears, apples and squash for their "new neighbors!" They were so incredibly happy, and so are we, as our friends will continue to live with protection!

# SASQUATCH HAS A SENSE OF HUMOR

By Teri and Jim Mattingly

We certainly didn't think it was funny at the time it happened, but looking back at it now, we have to laugh, especially when thinking how clever this animal was, and what kind of intelligence it would take for a wild creature to even conceive of such a diabolical deed!

It was after my husband and I had attended a seminar at our local university. Since we were retired faculty, we were often invited to attend an assorted number of topics that rotated through the various schools on the circuit.

This particular event was to be conducted by an associate of Doctor Jeffrey Meldrum from Idaho whom we had met at a seminar he held about fifteen years ago on the Sasquatch/Bigfoot animals that, at the time, we thought to be more of a joke on academia and a sort of tongue-in-check way to lighten up the serious curriculum that we lived with day in and day out.

Since that event so long ago, we had moved to northern California and ended up retiring here. You can imagine how shocked we had been at the point when we bought our home and our real estate agent casually brought up the subject of Bigfoot. I remember Jim rolling his eyes, and I reacted with something along the lines of "Save that crap for the tourists," and the poor realtor almost lost his cool! He apologized and then gave us a long explanation as to his being "totally honest with us," and after he finished, we both still doubted the creature's existence, just as we had at the two seminars we had attended, but having heard about the beings for a third time already, we decided to remain neutral on the subject. We ended up loving the home and no more "B.F. or B.S." came up.

That "neutral" stand existed until we were on a hike in the foothills of the mountain range near our home by the Pacific coast. A couple we had met a year before and with whom we had developed a friendship, had begun a new doctor ordered exercise regimen, and they invited us one day to accompany them. Then they explained that we were going "Squatchin'!" That statement drew a rapid, negative response from Jim, because the term was self-explanatory, and I intervened before he could answer, because his choice of words would possibly have been too forceful.

As I gave our friends an idea of our opinion as to the existence of such a creature in a carefully chosen manner, our friends quickly and laughingly changed their wording to "How about joining us for a hike?" To which we grinned widely and accepted gladly, because we hadn't ventured into the coastal range yet, other than at a couple of parks, and we frankly did not have any idea of where to begin.

We left early in our friends' four-wheel drive and we were soon in the beauty of a magnificent and very dark forest of monster pines. We were soon following our friends on a narrow trail that was obviously maintained by the state, as the thick brush rose high on both sides, and with the huge pine trees whose branches met above, the light came mainly from the opening up ahead where we anticipated a beautiful view of the ocean as we could hear the surf crashing not too far away from where we were.

Suddenly, the light ahead was almost totally extinguished, and we strained to see what we thought were more visitors returning, but the thought hit me that ours was the only vehicle in the parking area. Then the panic side of my brain lit up thinking perhaps it is a bear, and just as I was about to break the intense silence, a loud shout came from our friend as he shouted for us to get off the trail.

All four of us pushed into the thick brush, and as I turned to look back, a huge, hairy creature that I thought was a bear went crashing by; its enormous body causing a sweeping sound as the branches were smashed in all directions! As the beast rushed by me, it looked down at me, and I almost screamed as its golden eyes frightened me, but all I could do was gasp!

My breath was coming in gulps and Jim seemed to have turned a shade of white, and no one spoke until our friend did. The incident hadn't seemed to phase him, however his wife was pretty shook up.

As we recovered enough to walk to the light up ahead, our friend turned to face us with a wide grin on his lips, and said, "Now you've been Squatchin'!"

# TALK ABOUT IRONY!

## By Ella

*Publisher's Note: We received this story from a lady that photocopied it from a well-worn diary kept by her great grandfather.*

*Due to its reference to violence and death involving a Sasquatch, we were ready to reject it due to our criteria for acceptance, when something rang a bell with me. The item that gave this submission credibility and "rang my bell," was the gentleman's statement about being employed at an Oregon coal mine; I just knew that the man was being truthful, or at least up-front.*

*As I turned to my computer and typed in "Oregon coal mines," I had the shock of seeing on the first page, my own name! There before me was the article that I myself had written years ago when I was a real estate broker in Oregon. No wonder it sounded familiar, as I quickly remembered that I had been part of a blog where brokers campaigned nationally to attract people to move to our cities and states.*

*In this particular blog, I was advertising our recreational activities, and I was promoting our thousands of trails among our historic gold mines, and that our state also had trails to our seldom heard of coal mines. The promotions worked to attract many home buyers.*

*So here I sat, reading my own article and my ego wouldn't allow me to not accept this man's story as credible, because I could not conceive of anyone making up a story about anything as unexciting as a coal mine in Oregon.*

*It was interesting in the way the gentleman happened to end up at a coal mine, but he said he had been robbed shortly after he arrived in the coastal city of Coos Bay, and he lucked out in meeting the mine foreman who was in town recruiting.*

*From this point forward, we must defer to the translation from our submitter, as her great grandfather, Lars Nordgren, had kept his diary in his native Norwegian language, as she said, "Papa Lar's could speak English okay, but he never learned to write it, as he went to work after he got robbed of all his money.*

*We'll call our submitter Ella, and we thank her for translating her great grandfather's story, writing it in her own words, and submitting it to us.*

*University of Washington, Public domain, via Wikimedia Commons*

Lars was really down and out, because he had worked very hard for the last three years before he left his birthplace in Ostfold, Norway, and he had managed to save enough money to meet what the newspapers said the gold miners in California and Oregon reported was needed for a "stake." This stake was what a person would need at San Francisco prices to purchase the gold mining instruments like; shovel, pick and pan, plus several months of food sufficient to survive until a person had earned enough money to begin putting a pile of it in the bank. The word was, that Oregon had not yet become like California, and that there was still a lot of unexplored land available to just "stake your claim!"

Suddenly poor Lars was broke and couldn't even find a place to sleep when by chance, he heard a man speaking Norwegian to another man nearby, and he was overjoyed when they invited him to share a meal and a warm place to sleep.

As luck would have it, he heard that a mine foreman was at the local emporium looking to hire workers for a mine; and speaking just enough English to ask for a job, Lars signed his name to what he hoped to be a share of all the gold he envisioned.

Lars' first entry in his personal diary took an entire page of how devastated he had been to arrive after a day and a half on a rough riding, horse drawn wagon to find himself staring into a black hole where the only gold was in the seldom seen sunshine outside. This golden moment turned out instead, to be a coal mine; apparently he had heard it wrong. According to Lars journal, his almost daily entries showed the savings he began to accumulate, and having no place to spend any money except at the sparsely stocked company store, he seemed to become adjusted to his present situation, and he concentrated on accumulating more than he figured he would need in order to assure him of adequate funds to last until he struck it rich. He also learned to speak English thanks to several friends; at least enough to not end up on another misadventure.

One day, word came down that a team was needed to build a new mine building at a new and much more dense coal strike a couple of miles deeper into the mountains, and since the pay rate was a lot higher due to the rugged terrain in which it was located, Lars volunteered to be on the first team.

That was when it happened! There was over a week where there was not a single entry in Lars' diary, and then, there were four pages in a row.

Lars said that their crew of over twenty-five men had walked and ridden the crude trail into the valley below where their main operation was, and when they arrived in the small clearing at the bottom, there before them was a huge black mountain where the sides were solid with coal looking back at them.

They quickly made camp by erecting huge tents for temporary shelter, while teams of carpenters began erecting sleeping barracks and a mess hall, as the company was very concerned with keeping the men happy, to keep them from running off to the gold fields. There was a side-note that showed Lars kept pretending to be happy while his savings was getting close to where he could "head for the hills" himself.

The barracks building was soon built, and the coal mountain across the small valley soon had a giant entrance to its innards. The work went fast, as spring had also arrived, and the sun warmed everything up so every night was now pleasant, even the constant rains were warm.

Then events started happening. It all started about a week after a team had joined them from the main camp to speed up progress in what the company believed to be a higher grade of coal. Lars had no speculation as to what the reason was, because by that time he hated coal, and he joked in one notation that he couldn't even stand the smell of it anymore.

Then, there were no entries in Lars diary for about a week, but inserted in the diary were several notes on pieces of paper, written later and inserted. On one of them,

Grandfather said he had been out with a party of men pursuing a creature called "Lugaroo."

In another separate group of papers that Grandfather had evidently kept as a separate diary when he was in the hospital, and when he had recovered, he simply inserted them into the original diary rather than take all the time to rewrite the entries.

This separate set of notes talked about where a cook shack had been broken into one night, and some thieves had made off with huge bags containing frozen beef and chickens that were kept inside the large storage freezer, where hundreds of pounds of food sat in sand-covered ice. A fortune in foods had been looted at night, and the bosses had formed a large group of volunteers, of which Lars had eagerly joined.

The men were armed with some guns and lots of axe handles, as the management thought this would be sufficient to recover their food supplies from the Indian tribe they suspected had stolen the food.

The trail was easy to follow, as on one of the papers Lars had drawn a sketch showing a wide trail through mashed down branches leading to a series of crudely drawn teepees and some sort of dwellings made of stacked logs, like poorly constructed cabins.

Evidently, what the pursuers found at the trail's end was not an Indian village after all. Lars had vividly described that the tables had turned the minute all of the miners broke out of the forest to exact their revenge on the thieves, when they were met with a huge group of large, apelike creatures that suddenly swarmed over the miners, and pelted them with rocks, and pounded them with huge poles, and whipped at them with long willow branches.

Lars further stated that the few men who had guns had barely fired a few quick rounds before they fell first. The animals seemed to know that the ones carrying firearms were the most dangerous, as they went down right off.

Lars said that he had been hit hard with a thrown rock and his leg had broken in two places, so as he lay there in terrible pain, he witnessed the short battle, and the group of what we now call Sasquatch were totally gone, leaving the body-strewn field in a very few minutes after it all began.

Lars notes on this event were placed in the back of his diary. He eventually made it to the gold fields, and that's when he began a new diary.

*Publisher's Note: Ella mentioned on the phone to us that her great grandfather had never returned to Norway, but he married and stayed in Coos Bay, Oregon where she and her family live now.*

*In answer to our question as to whether Lars ever found gold, Ella said, "He found it in my grandmother!"*

# DAWN COMES TO SASQUATCH COUNTRY

By James Lindley

My name is John Lindley, and my wife Dawn and I recently moved to Sherwood, Oregon. Since we are retired, we came here to help Dawn's sister care for their mother as she is alone now.

We came up from Crescent City, California where I retired from my fishing business, and hopefully in the coming years, we may migrate to Arizona where we would like to live out our years without the gloom and rain.

The reason I am sending this letter is to tell you that we have been reading your Sasquatch books for several years now, and since we moved up here, we finally saw our second Bigfoot!

The first one, was in the National forest down by Brookings, but this last one was really up close and at "spittin' distance!" I mean that literally.

I should tell you first, that we like to target practice, and one of your books made reference to the fact that you had spent a lot of time shooting in the "Tillamook Burn." And on our first outing after moving here, we took our pistols and Dawn's father's old Jeep Wrangler and went into the ancient burn.

*An historical marker describing the Tillamook Burn*
*Visitor7, CC BY-SA 3.0 <https://creativecommons.org/licenses/by-sa/3.0>, via Wikimedia Commons*

After so many years after that devastating fire, the new growth trees have begun to dwarf the still standing spires of that horrendously devastating firestorm. Old timers in the area say the smoke could be seen from 500 miles out to sea!

*Creative Commons ~ Public Domain Photograph*

Dawn's mother said that she vaguely remembered the red skies at night, as she said she and her family watched from their home over in Washington State, and you could hardly see in the daylight due to a solid blanket of smoke.

Anyway, we followed the myriad of trails until we found exactly what I had hoped for; a road that led across an ancient logging bridge where I had to use the low-range four by four gear in order to climb the steep grade, and across the large planks of the ancient bridge. We doubted the road had seen much use over the years, as there were no signs of tire tracks, but we had walked it first before crossing, so we felt safe enough after we crossed. We soon were following the old ruts that were almost completely gone, and small saplings began to beat against our narrow front bumper, until at Dawn's urging, I finally quick smacking into them when the road we were on became quite narrow, and we were driving atop this narrow ridge line across what must have been a gorge with a stream rushing through it about fifteen feet below the dirt track and then up onto another old bridge. This one was narrow, but strong, and as we made it across, there was our ideal spot; a forested area that had sprouted in the midst of all the rotting timber, and from that point on, the entire area was beautiful as far as we could see. Thinking back to before we crossed that last bridge, we had no clue this area was here. It was like another world! One would never realize that there was a road anywhere nearby. It was no wonder it was so wild looking; much of it must have escaped that fire.

We made day camp under some magnificent pine trees and after eating and relaxing, we broke out the arsenal. Setting up targets at the base of a ridge further away across a meadow, where our expended bullets would hit into the side of the hill, we spent several hours just shooting at stones and weeds, where we could instantly see our hits and misses.

With the absence of any nearby residences, we burned up ammo with abandon, not caring about how long reloading them would take. Typical of shooters most everywhere, I left the piles of shotgun shells and the .22 caliber cases where they lay, which Dawn always frowned upon, but I got by with it. I think so anyway, but my bride has a way of somehow getting even for my tries at independence.

Call it pent up desire or just cabin fever, but out of one seven-day period we day camped on this spot five times! Then after a couple of rainy days, after all this is Oregon, we again woke with the sun and made our familiar way to our "private retreat" when Dawn made me stop just as we reached the point where I was about to make the downshift to the lower gear for the smooth climb over the bridge. She had me turn off the engine and on her way out, she beckoned me to follow, which out of curiosity, I was anxious to see what she was up to.

Dawn told me that something had been bothering her every time we came here, and today, she finally figured it out. Pointing at the road up to the wooden bridge, she still had me confused, and then she walked back to the track behind the Jeep and pointed, asking what I saw; to which I answered, "Tracks."

Then, following her becoming finger back to the road we were about to ascend, she pointed at the ruts leading up to the bridge and asked my why, since it had only been a couple of days, and there was plenty of evidence behind the Jeep of our repeated trips. Why there were no tracks further than where we now parked?

By then, we had reached the sand-covered planks crossing the creek, and as we continued walking across and down the other side, I could plainly see what I had failed to notice before. On the far side of that wooden structure there was absolutely no evidence of a tire track to be found anywhere!

I must have been standing with my mouth agape, because Dawn

told me to "close my mouth." She had figured it out, and then she led the way to where we usually parked and ate, and our signs were all over the place, as well as a littering of brass cartridge cases.

Then we put our heads together and concluded that something or someone had been only concerned with erasing our tracks; then it became apparent that something or someone had erased all sign of our having come up the trail and to keep the secret of there ever being a bridge there. This made perfect sense as humans, but what sort of animal would have such intelligence? Then, as if nature wished to provide evidence to support the fact that we had maybe "worn out our welcome." We sensed that whoever or whatever had erased our signs must have done so for their own protection.

Upon closer inspection on the walk back over the bridge, we were absolutely shocked when we saw a very large humanoid footprint in the wet sand where the creek passed under the wooden beams that held up the bulk of the bridge. At first, we were amazed at the size of the animal, and as our eyes followed the impressive tracks, we saw how serious these creatures had been; the main two supports that held up the heavy planks on the passenger side of the bridge had been somehow pushed off the base support beam below, and they were only holding up that entire side by about an inch of the very edge of the huge beam.

We looked at each other, and Dawn began to tremble uncontrollably as we both concluded that had we attempted to drive across, the weight of the Jeep would have most certainly caused the small bridge to collapse! As we held each other, we were both trembling, and as we stood there staring and trying to steady one another, off in the far distance, we both swore there were two large human-like shapes staring back at us. Then I glanced over to see Dawn give a wide wave and the creatures waved back! That really blew my mind, as I knew then that I was looking at my second sighting of Sasquatch.

As we drove back out of this area, I stopped several times to do my part in helping keep the secret by dragging a few dead trees onto the trail and rolling a few large rocks out on the ruts to really seal off that area, so others won't be as unthinking as we had been.

# NOT ALL SASQUATCH HIBERNATE

By Heidi Ogilvie

*Publisher's Note: Opinions from the other side came to us with reports that indicate the Sasquatch seems to be able to choose, or rather its metabolism allows it to adapt to varying weather conditions. This indicates that their systems can adapt to different climates, which explains why they are found most everywhere.*

*As we accept for publishing, stories that may stir controversy, such as the issue of hibernation, we feel it only fair to tell all sides of the story. Those submitters whose opinions are most often based on personal experiences, but that differ from others, that we have accepted for printing, may well be, correct in their opinions on the subject of hibernation among the Sasquatch, and it seems that there are two schools of thought on this subject. We believe that whether or not the Sasquatch hibernate may simply be a matter of their environment. Since these omnivores can vary their diets, it only makes sense that they can control more than that.*

*Since our own experiences with Sasquatch were during spring, summer and fall months, we are open to fact-based opinions where our story submitters have based their opinions on personal knowledge.*

*The story that follows is one from a couple who have contacted us in the past when they had their first Sasquatch sighting, and after their first full year in coastal Oregon, this is what they reported after getting to know their furry neighbors.*

We have lived nearby the Oregon coastal town of Yachats for a little over a year now and we began reading your Sasquatch books since we first arrived here.

Moving to this oceanside community was not in our plans, as we were perfectly happy in our home in Baker City, Oregon (on the far eastern side of the state), until my husband's uncle passed away and Jim was the sole heir to his property.

Being retired for a year already, we had my brother watch over our property in Baker and we came here to Yachats to sell the estate, which we figured would be only a matter of a month or so, and then we planned to return home to Baker City.

We soon found out that selling property on the dank and damp oceanside in the winter is like selling a field of freshly planted potatoes in anticipation of a super good crop to come later. You can tell people that show up to see the home all about the beautiful summers, but it's like trying to paint a masterpiece on a sheet of brown paper. To quote my husband, "That dog don't hunt!"

So, we had made the decision to move in to the house and wait out the dismally gray of a coastal winter. There was little sense in just sitting inside, so we bought some waterproof gear and began hiking the thick forests of the Pacific coast. We were surprised at how many really beautiful days there were among the rainy spells, and once we began to feel comfortable, we ventured even further into the thicker forests where there was an abundance of wild life.

Then we met Bigfoot! Although we were already pretty much convinced that this mystery animal really did exist as the locals had sworn to, it took an actual face to face meeting for us to truly believe. The Sasquatch was also said to be all over the area back home, but we had never seen one.

This chance meeting was when we were following a pine needle carpeted, wide trail among the jungle of enormous pine trees that wound circuitously through an enormous amount of fallen giants that had been uprooted years before by a huge storm that hit on one Columbus Day holiday that people from here to Portland still talk about.

Winds of one hundred plus miles an hour had virtually devasted many pristine forests that were already growing when Christopher Columbus first set foot on American soil. The cost of removal of the timber in this rugged area was, according to the locals, too great, so they left these magnificent monoliths to rot. After all of these years, the majority of these giants still seemed to be solid!

There were a lot of animal trails through this maze of monsters, and it took a few dead ends where the trees were on top of each other until we learned to follow the animal trails around and through where the forest dwellers had already found the easiest way to navigate the maze.

On the other side of this forest area that seemed to have borne the brunt of the main destruction was a place like a giant meteor hole or something, because it was over a hundred and fifty feet across and almost perfectly round, as though a gigantic rock had landed there and then bounced away.

We didn't bother with the cause, as this hole was perfect for our hobby; target shooting with handguns. After first discovering this perfect spot, we began coming here often, as we soon found out that a lesser-known truth about the Oregon coast is that, contrary to the common beliefs of visitors, it does not rain all the time, only a lot of the time! Oregon weather seems designed to keep the population low.

The nice thing about being retired here is that we could take advantage of the nice days and stay home on the rainy ones. You might say it's like being able to choose your own weekends. When the sun was out, so were we!

We'd buckle on our handguns, take a lunch, throw on our backpacks and head up into our private recreation area. The place we did our shooting was just over a big forested ridge, so it was unlikely that anyone in the residential areas could have ever even heard a gunshot.

One day after defeating our paper target foe, we were seated further down the hill from our target range and enjoying the sound of the small mountain stream (yes, we always wear hearing protection), but the sound of the gently falling creek seemed louder than it had before. Since we had not been this far down the slope, and had never given any thought to where the creek went after passing us, we decided to explore further since we seemed to be the only humans who ever came here.

There had been some heavy rains and a dusting of snow afterward that we figured was causing the increased sounds of splashing water, but as we descended further down the well-used animal trail, we heard a strange sound that reminded us of the snorting of the horses that we had recently ridden at a local ranch. That sort of a blow the horse makes as it lets off excess air when coming to a sudden stop.

We hadn't even thought of there being any other trails or routes into this area, so we were whispering back and forth what we each thought we heard, when suddenly, Jim's hand went up to signal a halt, and following his lead, I too knelt on the thick carpet of pine needles, and we peered at the stunning beauty of the sunlit mountain pond. Before and downhill from us, there was a sight I thought I would never see. There was a dark brown animal that at first, I thought was a bear, standing on its hind legs, but as it sniffed the air and slowly turned, it suddenly stopped dead still and stared directly at where we knelt, and even though neither of us had seen anything other than artist's renderings, I knew it was a Sasquatch!

As neither of us dared move, my breath coming in slight gasps, that to me were certainly loud, the animal made a glance to its left side and waved its giant paw, as one would to shoo away a pet, and then I saw another Sasquatch, only a much lighter brown and quite a bit shorter. The smaller animal carefully began sidestepping and then turned directly away, and carefully proceeded to make its way along the tumbling creek until it was hidden from our view. Only then did the larger animal make a slight turn, and before it too began leaving to follow its mate, it looked more closely at us, as if still trying to see if we were a danger, and then with a loud snort that seemed to be out of disgust at not knowing what we were, it bolted into the dark woods and was gone from sight in seconds!

Neither of us spoke at first as we listened to the retreating sounds of the Sasquatch seemingly smashing the forest in frustration. We sat down on the ground in a state of awe at these beautiful creatures that heretofore we had assumed to be only a tourist attraction, as no one we had met ever claimed to have seen one. We found out much later that most of the residents had, but they kept quiet, so more strangers wouldn't begin flooding in to their peaceful community.

This experience changed our regimen entirely. We no longer did any target shooting at our favorite place, but we still continued our hikes. Only now, we carried our larger caliber handguns, as we were curious about the Sasquatch, but ever mindful of the fact that it was still a wild animal; a huge, wild animal, and although we would never consider harming one of these creatures, the noise of a large caliber handgun should be a deterrent to most any animal. Some friends jokingly said that, "They carry guns as protection from Californians!"

After such an exciting experience, we shared our excitement with a couple of our newly made friends, being careful to not give away the place where the encounter happened, but it turned out that a couple of people whom we told, had also seen the creatures, but had not spoken of their events as they feared we might think they were fooling with us. Once they heard of our sighting, we learned that they were brimming with the desire to share their own tales; which they gladly did.

We soon found out that a large number of locals had similar stories that they were reticent about. After, we suddenly became "one of the group," the attitude of standoffishness to newcomers rapidly evaporated and we suddenly had a feeling of belonging, as though we had been born and raised here. It really seemed to be more of a home to us than where we had our roots clear across the state. Maybe because back in Baker, we all had ranches a way apart from one another.

We continued our weekly treks into the dense forests of "Sasquatch territory," and with suggestions from many of our new friends, we began a regimen of bringing gifts of food to our furry friends. Food items that people had found from experience that the Sasquatch seemed to really enjoy, and then the winter snows decided to dump tons of that cold, white blanket all over the mountains.

In the town of Yachats, the snow only lasted on the ground long enough to let us make a few passes with brooms, but the Sasquatch mountain retreat on the hills behind and around us were totally covered enough to remind us of being back in Baker City. The whole town of Yachats stayed white for awhile as the town didn't even own a snowplow. The state had plowed Highway 101 as it went from Canada to Mexico, and even though it was a two-lane road, to us it was our freeway.

Coming from a place where winters came to stay until spring, we were pleasantly surprised when it began to warm up, and combined with a slight, but enduring light rain (after all it is the Oregon coast), the snows up and down the coast became only a memory.

Up above town however was a different story. From the town, looking up at the white forest and slopes, we automatically assumed that we were socked in until spring. We made the assumption that the Sasquatch had retired to their dens or caves or whatever they and the bear population normally did back in eastern Oregon.

We were shocked to find out differently, and grudgingly accepted the invitation of a couple of our new friends to accompany them up on a road that led over to the other side of that mountain. On our jaunt, the day was sunny and the now seemingly warm ocean winds made the weather almost tolerable. We soon reached a place where the snowplows had cleared a wide area alongside the highway to allow plenty of room for the trucks crossing the mountains to put on or remove their tire chains.

Parking at the far end of the lot, our friends led us up into the thickly forested area that began at the very edge atop the cliff bordering where we parked.

The climb was strenuous, but after we reached the thick trees, it seemed as though the snow had failed to break through the thick canopy of pine boughs that covered the entire forest like a blanket.

The sun was fast melting the snow, and as it melted, it appeared that the water was running down the branches, and then down the trunks of the trees, so that walking beneath them was easy, as there was almost no snow on the forest floor, and the runoff down the tree trunks made it feel almost like a chilly summer day. We couldn't believe that it would be so peaceful and quite under the dark green canopy, and in places where there was an opening for the sun to shine through, there was a layer of steam rising in the air that augmented the pleasant smell of pine. Avoiding the occasional mound of accumulated snow that found its way through to the floor, there were wisps of steam rising as the sun's rays worked at melting it away.

The silence of the forest was hardly disturbed by the faint sounds of vehicles, and soon, the only sounds one would hear was the occasional thump of a pinecone as it fell to the carpeted forest floor. Even the sounds of the light wind seemed to disappear as our friends led us down a long sloping trail that exited the ridge line that we had been following, and after a few more twists and turns, we suddenly came to a stop, as our guide's hand raised above his head, and turning toward us he held his forefinger up to his lips as a signal to be still. We were both alarmed and excited at the same time!

Not even daring to do more than lightly breathe, we stood completely still while Ray, our host, took the "goody bags" we carried the whole time since we had parked. He had handed each of us a gunny sack which we accepted without question, as if we knew what they contained. We had correctly assumed from previous conversations where we were aware that these folks had been feeding the Sasquatch; no explanation was necessary.

Being one who likes to constantly chatter as we hike, I noticed that Jim was heeding the "rules of Squatchin'" that our friends referred to when our first discussion of the Sasquatch came about.

As the three of us stood silently by, our guide carefully and slowly walked down and around the huge boulder that stood as a silent sentry to guard the narrow trail he had taken, and as we stood without moving more than was necessary, after only a few minutes our guide returned, minus the four gunny sacks of treats for the Sasquatch.

We carefully and quietly returned the way we had come, and it wasn't until we reached the place where we had first entered the forest that anyone spoke a word. It was easy to understand the silence we had maintained, and our host explained that we were the first guests they had ever brought here, so they felt it best that we make the trip in silence, so as not to intimidate their Bigfoot friends, which we fully concurred with having recently experienced our own encounter and reacting the same way. The absolute excitement makes one feel protective of these awesome creatures!

During the entire winter, we made only three more visits to that area, the last trip being one where the guys had to fight their way through very deep snow in the forest. We ladies stayed at the parking area while the two goofy men brought the offerings to the Sasquatch. Jim was really surprised to see that when they arrived with the groceries that a giant of a Sasquatch came out of the darkness of the forest to take the bags before they were even out of sight.

Jim said they had turned to leave when a sort of whistle stopped them and they turned to see the huge "gorilla-looking" animal wave, and it again whistled as they in turn waved back to him. That emotional experience almost made Jim teary-eyed as he related that moment.

Keeping our word to not mention our friend's names, we were glad to protect their privacy, as they held important positions in the community; we wouldn't want to affect that.

We were so pleased to share the excitement and the knowledge of these Sasquatch, and we learned further from our friends that they suspected that the Sasquatch had a period of hibernation, but their opinions were mixed. On one hand, they were never able to make the trek much after mid-January, as they said that even the parking areas the we had used were not plowed on any kind of a regular basis after late January, and the snows were usually so deep at that summit at that time of the year, a person could not likely make the trek through the deep snow to that "rendezvous rock" anyway.

Our friends did not normally visit with more "friendship offerings" for those Sasquatch until April, so they could not definitely say whether the animals hibernated or not, but their consensus of opinion was that they believed that rather than hibernate, that the Sasquatch made their way back down to the lower altitudes, but they couldn't be sure, because the few dirt roads into the lower forests at that time of year were mostly mud. That was why they left their offerings at higher altitudes.

Well, our exciting experiences and the much shorter winters, had their affect on us. So, that next spring, we sold the home in Baker, Oregon and sunk our roots permanently in "Sasquatch Country," where we are currently making our lists of preferred Sasquatch cuisine, thanks to our friends.

We plan to give them a tour of our own Sasquatch area as it is much easier to get to since it's not too far from our back door and a heck of a lot more fun to visit.

# ABOUT THE AUTHORS

Upon retiring from larger cities, we sought the peace and quiet of the beautiful valley in which lay the city of Grants Pass, Oregon. Our move was a sort of destiny, as before graduating from high school, Gary had sat down with his parent's encyclopedias and a score of other books from the school library and began a search for a place he would like to live his life. His criteria was simple, as he knew it was not to be in his Minnesota birthplace, as the snow in winter and the mosquitoes in summer were definitely out.

After reading and studying until graduation, the place he had circled that best met his criteria was the small town of Grants Pass, Oregon. He said he never really thought he would ever go there, because he had never been further west than Denver, and the small town had no appeal, other than it best met his criteria; a valley surrounded by mountains, a city that seldom ever saw snow, it was close to major rivers and mountain lakes, deserts on the eastern edge of the area, and also the mountains and beaches of the Oregon coast. Also, the appeal of several designated wilderness areas appealed to him, and last of all, but possibly the most important of the whole bunch was no mosquitoes!

When we met in Portland, Oregon, we had both lived in many states and had traveled throughout the country from coast to coast. Ironically, we eventually retired to a place I had passed through many years before; Grants Pass, Oregon.

In retrospect, it seems like a prophecy fulfilled, as that was where we learned about what has become our hobby; Sasquatch!

Although we are now hiking the deserts of Southern Utah (my fault, I was tired of all the rain); we are still publishing the true-life stories from our still growing family of contributors in Sasquatch Country.

Additionally, we have been introduced to an entirely different subject that we have been carefully and cautiously studying. We were initially introduced to these creatures by some Native American friends of ours whom had made reference to the mystery surrounding both creatures, however the Skinwalker (Yee Naaldlooshii), as we view it, is pure evil! Not at all in the same category, except for the mystery surrounding both creatures is why we continue our research.

Thanks for the read!